VICTORY
in the
EYE GATE

Maria Vadia

Queenship
PUBLISHING COMPANY
P.O. Box 220 • Goleta, CA 93116
(800) 647-9882 • (805) 692-0043 • Fax: (805) 967-5133
www.queenship.org

Bible used unless specified:

Ignatius, The Holy Bible.
Revised Standard Version.
Catholic Edition. 1965, Ignatius Press, San Francisco.

Other Bibles used:

New American Bible.
St. Joseph medium size edition.
Catholic Book Publishing Company. 1986. New York, NY.

The New Jerusalem Bible.
Darton, Longman & Todd, Ltd. And Doubleday. 1985.

The Holy Bible, Douay Version.
P.J. Kenedy & Sons, New York. 1961.

Library of Congress Number # 2010930040

Published by:
Queenship Publishing
P.O. Box 220
Goleta, CA 93116
(800) 647-9882 • (805) 692-0043 • Fax: (805) 967-5133
www.queenship.org

Printed in the United States of America

ISBN: 978-1-57918-389-1

I dedicate this book to my precious Holy Spirit, who is the One responsible for the writing of this book.

I thank my dear sisters and brothers in the Lord who always pray for me. I ask the Lord to shower you with His love, joy and peace!

Maria Vadia has given us unique insight into the Eye Gate. For those who wish to progress in the spiritual life, this is a must read. "The eye is the lamp of the body, so if your eye is sound, your whole body will be full of light; but if your eye is not sound, your whole body will be full of darkness. If then the light in you is darkness, how great is the darkness." Matthew 6:22-23.

Victory in the Eye Gate unveils the many facets of our lives that must be transformed by the Holy Spirit if we are to truly walk with Jesus. Through scripture and from practical examples in her "spirit filled" life, Maria plumbs the depths of The Eye Gate in our lives.

Sister Linda Koontz S.N.J.M.

TABLE OF CONTENTS

"The eye is the lamp of the body. So if your eye is sound, your whole body will be full of light; but if your eye is not sound, your whole body will be full of darkness. If then the light in you is darkness, how great is the darkness!" (Matthew 6:22-23)

Beloved, there is a battle for our eyes! As the people of the kingdom, we need to surrender our eye gate to the Holy Spirit, so that we can see what the Lord is doing in our midst. We need to start seeing from His perspective. As temples of the Holy Spirit, we need to take possession of our eye gate and only allow what is of the Lord, what is beneficial and edifying to come into our spiritual house. As temples of the Holy Spirit and co-laborers with Him (2 Corinthians 6:1), we need to see with His eyes and from His perspective so that we can release the Lord's plans and purposes and see His kingdom extended on earth as it is in heaven. The Holy Spirit releases visions and dreams so that we can prophesy and partner with the Lord. On the day of Pentecost Peter quoted from the book of Joel:

"And in the last days it shall be, God declares, that I will
pour out My Spirit upon all flesh,
And your sons and your daughters shall prophesy,
And your young men shall see visions,
And your old men shall dream dreams…." (Acts 2:17).

Dreams and visions are part of our inheritance!

Jesus told His disciples

"…lift up your eyes, and see how the fields are already white for harvest." (John 4:35).

His agenda has not changed! He wants a harvest of souls to come into His kingdom and we are the harvesters! The Lord says to "lift up our eyes" from the difficulty, from the problem, from the trial, from the self-centeredness and instead focus on what He thinks is important: the harvest of souls!

Depending on how we use our eyes, we will be full of light or full of darkness. If full of light, we will be able to keep moving with the Holy Spirit, extending His kingdom, birthing His plans and purposes, producing good fruit and experiencing His glorious presence; if full of darkness, we'll be spiritually blind and miss what the Lord desires to do; we will not be a part of what He is doing today. We have a responsibility to use our eyes in the right way, because our eyes are a "gate" through which light and darkness, good and evil, can enter. After all, we are His ambassadors (2 Corinthians 5: 20) and we want to represent King Jesus effectively. Jesus says that we are the light of the world:

> "You are the light of the world. A city set on a hill cannot be hid. Nor do men light a lamp and put in under a bushel, but on a stand, and it gives light to all in the house. Let your light so shine before men, that they may see your good works and give glory to your Father who is in heaven." (Matthew 5:14-16).

The Lord is looking for "lamps!" For us to be light we must leave behind the ungodly ways of using our eyes and lift them up to the Lord. It is time for the church to wake up, to move from a spectator mentality to a co-laborer mentality! For too long we have been entertained and distracted by the world, sitting on the sidelines and warming the pews of the church while the enemy advances. Now is the time to enforce the victory of Calvary and destroy the "works of the devil." (1 John 3:8). One of the complaints the Lord had against the church of Laodicea, the lukewarm church, was that they were "blind" (Revelation 3:17). He counseled them to buy "salve to anoint your eyes, that you may see" (v.18). I say, "It's time to buy eye salve that we may see!"

Do you have a desire deep inside of you to be a part of what the Lord is doing today? Do you have a desire to see the body of Christ transformed into a beautiful bride? Do you have a desire to move in revelation, just like Jesus? Do you want to be a "living" lamp, releasing God's light, prophesying and setting the captives free? Do you want to extend God's kingdom on earth as it is in heaven by doing the works of Jesus? Do you want to enter into your prophetic destiny? Then the time is now to commit your eyes for God's purposes only.

LET'S PRAY:

"Father, I surrender my eyes to You, and to You only! I repent this day of the ungodly ways that I've used my eyes in the past. Forgive me for the unclean thoughts, the lusts of the eyes, pornography, useless daydreaming. I surrender not only my physical eyes but the eyes of my heart; sanctify my imagination and thought life. I realize it's Your desire that the eyes of my heart be opened so that I can see in the Spirit realm what Your plans are; it's Your desire that I co-labor with Your Spirit to extend Your kingdom on earth as it is in heaven. Lord I want to see like You see; I want to see through Your eyes; I want to see visions and dreams so that I can partner with You. Help me to see the "treasure" in people's hearts, to identify gifting and callings. Help me to set the captives free; I want to be a deliverer! Come, Holy Spirit, release vision and revelation into my life so that I can live out God's plan for my life."

Victory in the Eye Gate

I

"OUR NEED TO SEE!"

COME AND SEE!

"And He said to them, 'Come and see.'" (John 1:39).

This is a standing invitation from Jesus! He wants us to see! He wants us to see greater things than what we have seen! We need to understand that if we are not seeing in the Spirit we are blind! How can we co-labor with the Lord if we are spiritually blind? Jesus called the most religious group of Israel, the Pharisees, "blind guides" and "blind fools" in Matthew 23:16, 19. Is it possible for Church members that sing and help others be blind spiritually? Of course! All of us have spiritual blind spots that the Holy Spirit wants to remove so that we can see.

Jesus told Nathanael in John 1:50-51,

> "You shall see greater things than these. And he said to him, Truly, truly, I say to you, you will see heaven opened and the angels of God ascending and descending upon the Son of man."

He wants us to see; He wants us to see "greater things!" He wants us to see into the Spirit realm so that we can partner with Him and co-labor with the Holy Spirit. The promise of an open heaven is for us too, not just for Nathanael! He wants us to see and experience heaven opened over our lives. This is part of our inheritance and we need it to carry on with Jesus' works. We are to contend for an open heaven as we follow Jesus; this means walking on earth with full access and release of the blessings of the kingdom, including an unhindered relationship with the Father so that we can see what Papa is doing and become fruitful sons and daughters. An open heaven is heaven invading earth, it's His manifest presence in our midst! This is how Jesus taught us to pray "let Your Kingdom come, let Your will be done on earth as it is in heaven." Under an open heaven we have everything we need to destroy the works of the devil and extend His kingdom on earth; we have access to His voice, healing, power, angels, goodness, miracles, signs, wonders, joy, peace, love, deliverance, etc. There is no lack in His kingdom when His glory is released!

Jesus was the One that opened heaven for us through the power of the Cross, when He triumphed over the powers and the principalities (Colossians 2:15). He resurrected and ascended back into glory and gives to us the open heaven. This is our inheritance! Heaven opened over Jesus when He was baptized in the river Jordan:

> "And when Jesus was baptized, He went up immediately from the water, and behold, the heavens were opened and he saw the Spirit of God descending like a dove, and alighting on him; and lo, a voice from heaven saying 'This is my beloved Son, with whom I am well pleased.'" (Matthew 3:16-17).

I believe that an open heaven becomes a reality for us when we are baptized in the Holy Spirit, because the "eyes of our hearts" become enlightened (Ephesians 1:18) to see the reality of what the Lord has done for us. In other words, through the immersion in the Holy Spirit our spiritual eyes are opened so that we can take full possession of the inheritance that Jesus won for us in Calvary, including an open heaven!

This is what Peter experienced in Acts 10 at a crucial moment in the history of God's people, when the Lord wanted to take the Gospel to the Gentiles. A good Jew would never go to the house of a Gentile; and now heaven opened over Peter as he was praying. The same vision was given to him three times because the

Lord had to break through and change Peter's way of thinking:

> "...Peter went up on the housetop to pray...and he became hungry and desired something to eat; but while they were preparing it, he fell into a trance and saw heaven opened...." (Acts 10:9-11).

Because of this revelation Peter went to the house of Cornelius, a Gentile, to proclaim the good news! In Cornelius' house, the Holy Spirit came as Peter preached on all these Gentiles who heard the Word; they spoke in tongues and were baptized. How could the Lord change Peter's mind and make this visit possible? It started with an open heaven and a vision given to His servant Peter, as he prayed.

Even surrounding the birth of the Messiah, Luke 2:8-20, this is how the Lord got the message across to the shepherds to go and see Baby Jesus. In those days shepherds didn't count much, but not from God's perspective! The shepherds experienced an open heaven:

> "And an angel of the Lord appeared to them, and the glory of the Lord shone around them...." (v.9).
> "And the angel said to them...." (v.10).
> "And suddenly there was with the angel a multitude of the heavenly host praising God and saying...." (v.13).

What was the result of this experience of an open heaven?

> "When the angels went away from them into heaven, the shepherds said to one another, 'Let us go over to Bethlehem and see this thing that has happened, which the Lord has made known to us.' And they went with haste...." (Luke 2:15-16).

In early 1989, in response to my many cries to the Lord to "Take me places where I can tell people about Jesus,!" the Lord took me to a home for the homeless with AIDS. I went to that home totally unaware of where I was going; truly, I would have never gone there on my own, but a sister in the Lord took me there. I was shaking on the inside as I stepped into a courtyard; but suddenly, heaven opened and I heard the choirs of angels singing and rejoicing. I sat down in a bench to absorb what I was hearing, and I heard the voice of the Lord telling me "Welcome, this is where I want you." From that moment I knew that the Lord Himself had taken me there; I faithfully served the Lord there for fifteen years, until the place shut down. At times the enemy created opposition to our ministry, but I never doubted or wavered whether I was supposed to be there, because the Lord Himself had taken me there and had confirmed it! Many people asked me "Aren't you afraid to get the HIV virus?" I had no fear because the Blood of Jesus is more powerful than any virus! We saw hundreds of individuals turn their lives over to Jesus, with great miracles of healing as well. Alleluia!

In 2007 when the first WOW (Women of Worship) conference was about to take place, I received an unexpected phone call that the worship leader would not be able to make it. After the initial shock, I finally started to lift up my eyes to the Lord, knowing that He had a plan. One day as I was praying in the Spirit for the conference, I saw heaven opened and angels descending on a ladder with all sorts of musical instruments! The Lord was saying "I will send My angels to help with the praise and worship. Don't worry." From that moment on I knew everything would be okay, and it was! We were able to worship Papa in spirit and in truth (John 4:23-24), and truly there was a heavenly, angelic presence that released great joy and freedom to those present! Thank You, Jesus!

Should it surprise us that the Lord sends angels to help us carry on with His works? Of course not! They are "ministering spirits sent forth to serve, for the sake of those who are to obtain salvation." (Hebrews 1:14). The angels ministered to Jesus throughout His earthly ministry, as well as to His followers in the early church. When there is an open heaven, the ministry of angels abounds. This year as I was ministering in Wellington, New Zealand, I sensed that a cold was trying to come against me. As we were worshiping the Lord, I saw in the spirit an angel standing in front of me with a pot of honey and a spoon in his hand. He had come to give me "medicine" against the cold. In faith I opened my mouth and took the honey; I never got sick!

In the summer of 2008 in Winthrop, Massachusetts, Father Tom DiLorenzo left town and left me "in charge" of his radio program. I love to speak on the radio, but I am not technically inclined. I had no idea of how to work all the switches and knobs and I was freaking out. I had to sit down with Father Tom and write down every single step of what was needed to be done for the radio program to be broadcasted. I was worried, fearful, anxious, acting like an orphan! In the morning of the broadcast, as I woke up, heaven opened over my life and I heard all of heaven singing a song to me, with many musical instruments. I heard the choirs of angels and they sang a message to me twice, that went like this:

> "The Holy Spirit, the Holy Spirit, does it all! The Holy Spirit, the Holy Spirit does it all!"

I understood more than ever that when we say YES to what the Lord is asking of us, it's a matter of flowing in the rivers of the Spirit! It's all done, we just need to enter in and step into those good works (Ephesians 2:10) by faith! Now I always thank the Lord for an open heaven over my life!

Another example of an open heaven in the Scriptures is found in Acts 7:54-56, when Stephen is stoned to death by the religious authorities of his day. As Stephen's persecutors became enraged at him, this is what happened:

> "But he, full of the Holy Spirit, gazed into heaven and saw the glory of God, and Jesus standing at the right hand of God; and he said, 'Behold I see the heavens opened, and the Son of man standing at the right hand of God.'"

Powerful! Stephen "gazed" into heaven in the midst of the attack to see something much greater than his circumstances: he saw the glory of God! This enabled him to endure the stoning and pray for his persecutors with a loud voice:

> "Lord, do not hold this sin against them." (v.60).

In Revelation 4:1, John saw an open door in heaven and a voice inviting him to go up:

> "After this I looked, and lo, in heaven an open door! And the first voice, which I had heard speaking to me like a trumpet, said, Come up hither, and I will show you...."

This is an invitation for believers to go up through that open door and allow the Lord to show us what we need to know for such as time as this! As co-laborers with the Holy Spirit, we need a download of revelation so that we can partner effectively with the Lord to carry on with His works! (John 14:21).

> "To thee I lift up my eyes, O thou who art enthroned in the heavens!" (Psalm 123:1).

GIVE ME 20/20 VISION, LORD!

> "He who says he abides in him ought to walk in the same way in which he walked." (1 John 2:6).

Brothers and sisters, we need to "look" at Jesus! He is our model! We need to focus on Him. We have been predestined to be conformed to His image (Romans 8:29); so to Him we must look to be transformed. As we behold Him, we are

> "changed into his likeness from one degree of glory to another; for this comes from the Lord who is the Spirit." (2 Corinthians 3:18).

We want to look like Him, walk like Him, love like Him, speak like Him. We must go to the Scriptures to see how he walked! We need a "kingdom mentality." He walked in revelation; because

He walked in revelation, He walked in power and love, manifesting the heart of the Father.

Let's look at Jesus' words:

> "Jesus said to them, Truly, truly, I say to you, the Son cando nothing of his own accord, but only what he sees the Father doing; for whatever he does, that the Son does likewise. For the Father loves the Son, and shows him all that he himself is doing; and greater works than these will he show him, that you may marvel." (John 5:19-20).

It should be our desire to live just like Jesus, only doing what we see our Father do! I believe that this is the Father's desire for us: that we do only what we see Him do. What does it take? A love relationship! Jesus said in John 14:21,

> "He who has my commandments and keeps them, he it is who loves me; and he who loves me will be loved by my Father, and I will love him and manifest myself to him."

When we are in love with Jesus, everything changes! When we are in love, we want to please the other person; when we are in love with Jesus, we want to please Jesus! It's not about following a set of rules of do's and don'ts. It becomes our desire to do things His way; not because we have to, but because we want to! When we love Jesus "his commandments are not burdensome" (1 John 5:3). It becomes a joy to obey Him and be a doer of His Word! (James 1:22). We receive a "new heart" and with this new heart it's our desire to please Him (2 Corinthians 5:9). So what flows from this love relationship according to Jesus in John 14:21? Revelation! An unveiling of Who He is! An ever-increasing manifestation of His glory! The eyes of our hearts will start opening and "seeing" new things; He will reveal to us the depths of His heart and will start showing us what His plans are. This is an ongoing process, not a just one time thing; as we are faithful with the small, He will release more and more revelation to draw us into a deeper intimacy with Him for His plans to be accomplished in us and through us.

Jesus said in John 14:12-14,

"Truly, truly, I say to you, he who believes in me will also do the works that I do;
And greater works than these will he do, because I go to the Father.
Whatever you ask in my name, I will do it, that the Father may be glorified in the Son;
If you ask anything in my name, I will do it."

As God's people, we are supposed to be doing the "greater works." We know that Jesus healed the sick, resurrected the dead, casted out demons, moved in miracles, walked on water, etc. The Lord says that we are to be doing even greater works! As believers we are "earthen vessels" who carry a great treasure inside of us! (2 Corinthians 4:7) We just need to let Him out! As we do, there will be an expansion of His kingdom as His power is released through us to set the captives free. We are to think big so we can ask big and receive big, and in this the Father is greatly glorified. We have been anointed to "destroy the works of the devil" (1 John 3:8) just like Jesus! We are to enforce the victory of Calvary into every situation that is not conformed to God's word and will. It's time for us to rise up and proclaim the gospel of the kingdom, manifesting it's power,

"For the kingdom of God does not consist in talk, but in power." (1 Corinthians 4:20).

Do you think that it is possible that we miss God's plan for our generation because we are not "seeing?" Of course! Can you hear the cry of the lost?

"The harvest is past, the summer is ended, and we are not saved." (Jeremiah 8:20).

Recently, as my friend and I were leaving another friend's house, we encountered just outside the door of her house a young man that looked confused, upset, disoriented. He had no shoes on, his pants were ripped; he reminded me of a wounded animal! It looked like he was on the run. I saw in the Spirit that the Lord wanted us to help him; he was not there by accident, but the Lord Himself had brought him to us in the perfect timing of the Holy Spirit! In the natural, we should have run away from him! He could not respond appropriately to any question asked. Apparently there was a lot of trouble at home, especially with his step-father. I thought, "Another human being carrying a Father-wound!" I was broken thinking of this young man's mother, and how if I was his mother I would like someone to help him. The Lord reminded me of this Scripture:

> "And as you wish that men would do to you, do so to them." (Luke 6:31).

Our hearts were broken for this young man! I said, "Son, only Jesus can save, heal and restore you and He loves you ." This young man said he knew Jesus; I laid hands on him for healing and prophesied over his life. I saw in the Spirit that this young man was very talented musically. We spoke and prophesied life, healing, restoration over him. I knew in the Spirit that the Lord Himself had brought this young man to us, so that we could minister prophetically to him. I spoke with his mom and we dropped him off at a nearby hospital. You see, faith involves taking a risk; we had to look beyond the natural not only to minister to this young man the blessings of the Kingdom, but to take him inside my car! This young man could have had a knife or gun, but the blood of Jesus is more powerful than any human weapon! But greater is He that lives in me than he who is in the world! (1 John 4:4). Brothers and sisters, we have been anointed to

> "...bind up the brokenhearted, to proclaim liberty to the captives, and the opening of the prison to those who are bound...." (Isaiah 61:1).

Where are the brokenhearted, the captives, the bound? Everywhere! Open your eyes and release the kingdom! Jesus expects us to have our eyes opened to the people He brings to us. In Matthew 25:31-46, He talks about judgment day and the need to "see," so that we can feed the hungry, give drink to the thirsty, welcome the stranger, clothe the naked, visit the sick and imprisoned. Jesus was asked

> "Lord, when did we see thee hungry and feed thee, or thirsty and give thee drink? And when did we see thee a stranger and welcome thee…." (v.37-39).

Jesus said,

> "Truly, I say to you, as you did it to one of the least of these my brethren, you did it to me." (v.4).

To carry on with His works, He has given us the Holy Spirit; we are not orphans!

> "Not by might, nor by power, but by my Spirit, says the Lord of Hosts." (Zechariah 4:6).

I like what David wrote in Psalm 16:8,

> "I keep the Lord always before me; because he is at my right hand I shall not be moved."

David's eyes were focused on the Lord; the presence of the Lord in David's life was more real than anything he could see with his natural eyes. Therefore, he did not fear!

Last year in a parish in Kampala, Uganda, located in a very busy area, we were holding daily meetings for a week. One morning as we were praising and worshiping the Lord, a young man unexpectedly walked up to us in the front of the Church; he simply took our flags and started to praise the Lord next to us. At times he would grab our hands to praise the Lord together. Quite frankly, his behavior was inappropriate. To make matters worse, this young man looked absolutely terrible; he smelled bad, hair uncombed, shirt opened, barefoot. By the grace of God, as I looked inside his heart, the Lord showed me that he had a heart for God. I told the Lord, "I'm just flowing in the rivers of Your Spirit! I am not going to tell this young man anything; I will keep praising You!" When praise and worship ended, the leader of the prayer group gently took this young man apart and ministered deliverance and healing to him. Two days later, the same young man came back! This time he looked totally different: he was dressed nicely, hair combed, clean, with shoes on. He gave testimony of what had happened to him: his father had taken him to the witchdoctor for some business transactions, but he ran away not wanting anything to do with the witchdoctor. This young man said, "I ran away from the witchdoctor's house as fast as I could and came to the nearest Catholic Church seeking refuge!" I was so thankful to the Holy Spirit that I had "seen" correctly and by God's grace acted on what I had been shown! Do you see how important it is to receive revelation from the Holy Spirit so that we can co-labor together and bring in the harvest? Do you see how important it is that we receive those that the Lord brings to us, in spite of how they look or smell?

> "But my eyes are toward thee, O Lord God; in thee I seek refuge...." (Psalm 141:8).

NEEDED: MORE REVELATION OF THE FATHER!

> "All things have been delivered to me by my Father; and no one knows the Son except the Father, and no one knows the Father except the Son and any one to whom the Son chooses to reveal him." (Matthew 11:27).

To know the Father comes by revelation! It is Jesus who reveals the Fatherhood of God; He reveals the heart of the Father. Jesus said in John 12:45,

> "He who sees me sees him who sent me."

Jesus told Philip in John 14:9,

> "...he who has seen me has seen the Father."

One more reason to focus on Jesus! He is the revelation of Who the Father is! Jesus told His Father in John 17:6,

> "I have manifested thy name to the men whom thou gavest me out of the world…."

The truth is that many of God's children have a "father wound" that needs to be healed. Many have suffered abuse, neglect, abandonment, lack of love and affirmation, etc., from their earthly fathers, so trusting in their heavenly Father becomes almost impossible. The enemy loves to destroy the father image for this reason, knowing that it will be very difficult for people to trust in God as Father. Many have an "orphan spirit" on them, which causes them to live, think and act like orphans. This, I believe, is one reason that Jesus told His disciples in John 14:18,

> "I will not leave you orphans; I will come to you." (NAB).

He was talking about the Holy Spirit! The Holy Spirit indwells believers, empowering us and releasing every good gift we need to carry on with the business of the kingdom. He is our helper! He is our comforter, our teacher, the Spirit of wisdom and revelation, the Spirit of truth and much more! He is the one that pours the love of God into our hearts (Romans 5:5).

The revelation of the Father is necessary to live a secure and victorious life on earth. In the Father we are secure, loved, protected, provided for. He has already provided everything that we need so that we can fulfill our destiny in Him. Ephesians 1:3 says,

> "Blessed be the God and Father of our Lord Jesus Christ, who has blessed us in Christ with every spiritual blessing in the heavenly places, even as he chose us in him before the foundation of the world…."

As children of the Father, we have been blessed with every spiritual blessing that we need. It gives great comfort to know that the Father chose us even before the foundation of the world was laid. Awesome! We are not in this planet by accident, we are not one more number! We have been knitted in our mothers' wombs by Him:

> "For thou dist form my inward parts, thou didst knit me together in my mother's womb." (Psalm 139:13).

> "Thy eyes beheld my unformed substance; in thy book were written, every one of them,
> The days that were formed for me, when as yet there was none of them." (Psalm 139:16)

Does not Jesus say in Luke 12:32 that Papa has given us the kingdom? He says,

> "Fear not, little flock, for it is your Father's good pleasure to give you the kingdom."

He gives the kingdom to us because we belong to Him! He loves us! He says, "Fear not!" You see, if we truly believed and trusted the Lord, things like jealousy, fear, anxiety, competition, strife, would not play a role in our lives! Why? Because the Father not only has already provided for every need, but He has a specific purpose and plan for every son and daughter:

> "For I know the plans I have for you, says the Lord, plans for welfare and not for evil, to give you a future and a hope." (Jeremiah 29:11).

As I travel and proclaim the Word of God, I have seen that most of God's children do not know what their mission in this planet is. The Church is suffering from an identity crisis and this I believe is a big reason why the Church today is not operating at full strength! The people of God have no vision for their mission! (Proverbs 29:18). This is absolutely tragic, because as God's children we are all part of the body of Christ. Imagine a human body whose lungs, heart, intestines, etc. do not know what its function is! That body would be in intensive care, being kept alive artificially! In many ways this is the state of the Church; most of its members are just Church attendees, spectators, with no relationship with the Lord, no revelation of the heart of the Father and no vision for their lives on this planet. This is one reason the enemy has been able to penetrate and push his agenda in so many arenas in this nation! The Church is asleep! There is a correlation between a sleepy, lethargic, prayerless Church and the increase of evil in society. Just look at the increase of New Age, the psychic businesses and occult involvement in this nation! What does this say to us? People are hungry and searching for meaning and truth and they have not found it in our parishes and prayer groups, so they flock to the wrong places searching for answers! Brothers and sisters, we have the TRUTH: JESUS! I say "It's time to wake up!"

The Lord does not want us to live a life of lack, fear, worry or anxiety; this will keep us focused on the wrong things. He wants us to have a kingdom mentality. Jesus says in Matthew 6:31-33,

> "Therefore do not be anxious, saying, What shall we eat? Or What shall we drink? Or What shall we wear? For the Gentiles seek all these things; and your heavenly Father knows that you need them all. But seek first his kingdom and his righteousness, and all these things shall be yours as well."

Jesus says that our Father is the provider. The key to provision is to put the kingdom first and his righteousness, and then whatever we need will be supplied by Abba (Matthew 6:33). When we put King Jesus first and the interests of His kingdom, everything that we need will be supplied by Papa. There is no lack in God's kingdom; the world's financial system might be cracking, but the kingdom of God cannot be shaken! Hebrews 12:28 says,

> "Therefore let us be grateful for receiving a kingdom that cannot be shaken...."

2009 began with a lot of "bad" news in the political and economic arenas. The media made matters worse by creating an atmosphere of fear and uncertainty. As I sought the Lord, He spoke to me just the opposite! He said 2009 is the year of expansion, enlargement and increase. WOW! In the midst of a financial crises, the Lord was telling me to get ready to expand. Isaiah 54:2-3 says,

> "Enlarge the place of your tent, and let the curtains of your habitations be stretched out; hold not back, lengthen your cords and strengthen your stakes. For you will spread abroad to the right and to the left…."

I stood on that Word, believing it and trusting the Lord to see it come to pass. With expectant faith, I saw how four new countries opened to me! Already this year I have been to all four new countries to proclaim His Word and Papa has provided for everything! I said yes, and the provision came. Amen!

> "Now to him who by the power at work within us is able to do far more abundantly than all that we ask or think, to him be glory in the church…." (Ephesians 3:20).

RELATIONSHIP RELEASES REVELATION!

It's relationship that He wants with each one of us; this means spending time with Him in praise, adoration and worship, prayer, and in His Word. We need to have a heart like Mary of Bethany and sit at His feet and be fed by Him. Martha, Mary's sister, had the same opportunity that Mary had, to spend time with Jesus, but she was "distracted," anxious and troubled. She chose instead to get busy with serving while the Master was speaking and teaching in her own living room! There is nothing wrong with serving the Lord, but at that moment, Martha was unable to "see" what was best! Because she didn't "see," she could not make the right choice. Jesus told her,

> "Martha, Martha, you are anxious and troubled about many things; one thing is needful. Mary has chosen the good portion…" (Luke 10:41-42).

Mary of Bethany is a beautiful prophetic picture of what the Lord desires in each one of us: to keep our eyes on Him at all times! Mary had the eyes of a "dove." (The interesting thing about doves is that they focus on one thing at a time, without distraction. They have no peripheral vision).

> "Behold, you are beautiful, my love; behold, you are beautiful; your eyes are doves." (Song of Solomon 1:15).

No wonder it was Mary that had the revelation to anoint Jesus before the Passover! While the rest were sitting having dinner (with Martha serving!), Mary showed up with a,

> "pound of costly ointment of pure nard and anointed the feet of Jesus and wiped his feet with her hair; and the house was filled with the fragrance of the ointment." (John 12:3)

The disciples were baffled and could not understand what in the world Mary was doing! Judas got angry at her for spending so much money on Jesus (John 12:4-5) and the others were "indignant" for the same reason (Matthew 26:8). But Mary had sat at His feet and had listened to His Words and she simply put into practice what she heard and believed. She had revelation that the others did not have! Jesus said,

> "My mother and my brethren are those who hear the word of God and do it." (Luke 8:21).

> James says, "But be doers of the word, and not hearers only, deceiving yourselves." (James 1:22).

Mary had a "holy" boldness to do what pleased the Lord and not be intimidated by what others thought or said about her. She just wanted to please her Lord. Because she had the "eyes" of a dove, her eyes were fixed only on the Lord. Keeping our eyes on Jesus and having intimacy with Him releases a holy boldness that is needed today so that others may see that Jesus is truly alive!

This is the boldness the early Church manifested! In Acts 4:13 the Jewish authorities were amazed at the boldness of Peter and John:

> "Now when they saw the boldness of Peter and John, and perceived that they were uneducated, common men, they wondered; and they recognized that they had been with Jesus."

What is the key to the victorious, Christian life? To be with Jesus! Jesus said,

> "I am the vine, you are the branches. He who abides in me, and I in him, he it is that bears much fruit, for apart from me you can do nothing." (John 15:5).

If we are going to be fruitful and co-labor with the Holy Spirit, we need to spend time with Jesus! This is the time to be like the "wise maidens" (Matthew 25:1-13); this is the time to store in our heavenly bank account vast reserves of prayers that will be activated at the right time! Jesus says,

> "Do not lay up for yourselves treasures on earth, where moth and rust consume and where thieves break in and steal, but lay up for yourselves treasures in heaven...." (Matthew 6:19-20).

There are no shortcuts! When we pray, Jesus said that "...your Father who sees in secret will reward you." (Matthew 6:6).

As we spend time with the Lord, the Holy Spirit Himself will reveal to us what we need to know! This will help us walk by faith and not by fear! Jesus said in John 16:13,

> "When the Spirit of truth comes, he will guide you into all the truth; for he will not speak on his own authority, but whatever he hears he will speak, and he will declare to you the things that are to come."

One "Word" from the Lord changes our perspective! It releases faith, light, revelation, clarity, strength, power!

I remember my first trip to Tanzania to teach at a seminar. This was not a weekend seminar, but a three week seminar! Morning, noon and night, except for Mondays! The Lord gave me revelation through a vision and this is what I saw:

I saw myself drawing from my "wells" of the Spirit beautiful pearls! The Lord was showing me that precious "pearls of revelation" would be drawn out of His rich deposit in me to feed His people. What was the result of this vision? Great peace and joy in my assignment in Tanzania! As I responded to His Word in faith, I was able to flow in the rivers of His Spirit with great results! The Lord is faithful and true to His Word: He always supplies what we need as we put His kingdom first! (Matthew 6:33). The students were blessed and even today I still hear of "praise reports" in their service to the Lord!

Once again, after the death of Lazarus, it was Mary who obtained a resurrection from Jesus. She knew how to touch His heart! I believe that as Mary sat at the feet of Jesus she "caught" revelation that others missed. Both Martha and Mary told Jesus the same thing:

> "Lord, if you had been here, my brother would not have died." (John 11:21; 32).

The difference between Martha and Mary is that when Mary saw Jesus, she

> "fell at his feet, saying to Him…." (John 11:32).

Mary worshipped! She had the heart of a worshiper! In the midst of her pain and tears, she was still able to put Jesus first and worship Him! This touched His heart and she got a resurrection!

We are living in times where there has been an acceleration of the Holy Spirit, and we are alive for such a time as this! The Holy Spirit is raising up champions like David and Mary of Bethany, people that have been spending time with Jesus, unseen and unnoticed by others, but certainly known by God! David is also a prophetic type for these times; a shepherd boy in the middle of nowhere taking care of sheep. In that hidden place of solitude, he developed a relationship with the Lord and learned to trust and rely on Him. Nobody knew this, however, except God! His family was unaware of David's relationship with the Lord; when the prophet Samuel came to Jesse's house to anoint the next king of Israel, Jesse (David's father) didn't even bother to tell David to show up! (1 Samuel 16).

In 1 Samuel 17, when the Israelite and Philistine armies were facing each other, David was sent there by his father to take cheese and bread to his brothers. However, God had another plan for David being there: to slay Goliath! The entire Israelite army feared the giant, except David. What was the difference between David and the rest of the Israelite warriors? David knew the Lord intimately! No matter how big and intimidating Goliath looked, David's God was bigger! In Psalm 16:11 David wrote,

> "I keep the Lord always before me; because he is at my right hand I shall not be moved."

David had made a choice to always "see" the Lord before Him and therefore he was not afraid of a giant. David "saw" from God's perspective. He said,

> "The Lord who delivered me from the paw of the lion and from the paw of the bear, will deliver me from the hand of this Philistine." (1 Samuel 17:37).

David had a history with the Lord; he knew he could call on the Lord and trust Him to deliver him, just as He had done previously with the lion and the bear. Do you have a personal history with the Lord? It's in that place of intimacy that you receive a download from heaven and you start seeing from His perspective. Every battle, difficulty or trial you have gone through has been a preparation for you to become a "giant slayer!" See it from God's perspective: you are "more than a conqueror " (Romans 8:37) and you have been seated in the heavenly places in Christ Jesus (Ephesians 2:6)!

"Far above all rule and authority and power and dominion, and above every name that is named, not only in this age but also in that which is to come; and he has put all things under his feet...." (Ephesians 1:21-22).

II

LORD, GIVE ME A NEW SET OF EYES!

> "He who walks righteously and speaks uprightly, who despises the gain of oppressions,
> Who shakes his hands, lest they hold a bribe, who stops his ears from hearing of bloodshed,
> And shuts his eyes from looking upon evil, he will dwell on the heights;
> His place of defense will be the fortresses of rocks; his bread will be given him,
> His water will be sure. Your eyes will see the king in his beauty; they will behold a land that stretches afar." (Isaiah 33:15-17).

Brothers and sisters, our eyes were created for God's glory! We are to "dwell on the heights" and see from His perspective. It was after the Apostle John was carried to " a great, high mountain" that he was able to see the Bride of Christ in all her beauty:

> "...Come, I will show you the Bride, the wife of the Lamb. And in the Spirit he carried me away to a great, high mountain, and showed me the holy city Jerusalem coming down out of heaven from God, having the glory of God, its radiance like a most rare jewel, like a jasper, clear as crystal." (Revelation 21:9-11).

It was from "a great, high mountain" that John's perspective changed; it was there that he saw from God's perspective. John was not necessarily having a great time in the island of Patmos, where this "revelation" took place. He was forced to go there as an exile because of his faith! Patmos was a penal island. He was in Patmos

> "...on account of the word of God and the testimony of Jesus." (Revelation 1:9).

It was after the fall of man that Adam and Eve became self-conscious, trapped by "self" and realized they were naked; before that they were just God-conscious. Before the fall their eyes were focused on the Lord; but after the fall their eyes became focused on self. The "I, me, myself" syndrome took control of our lives. The Lord wants to "recapture" our eyes so that we can see as He sees! For the Lord to recapture our eyes we need to surrender and live for Him. He must capture our hearts! Our eyes must be washed with "two waters":

> "The water of the Word" (Ephesians 5:26);
> "The rivers of living water, the Holy Spirit" (John 7:38).

Another way to understand what I'm trying to say is that the Word of God and the Holy Spirit must become the "filter" through which we see, so that we can see as God sees. Like the blind man whom Jesus healed in John 9, we must "wash" our eyes in order to see. After this man gained his sight, people said of him:

> "...Is not this the man who used to sit and beg?" (John 9:8).

We are not beggars! We have to "wash" our eyes in order to see that we are Christ's body on earth, chosen, anointed, equipped, authorized to fulfill the Great Commission. There is a purpose and a plan for why we are here on planet earth: to extend His kingdom "on earth as it is in heaven!" The Lord has already given to us everything that we need to carry out His command. Stop begging and start commanding! Release your God-given, delegated authority over the powers of darkness (Luke 10:19)!

There must be a convergence of our physical eyes with the eyes of our heart. We must give up ungodly ways of using our eyes, which is intended to be a gate through which revelation comes in. We cannot expect the Lord to bless us with His secrets and revelation if we are indulging in sinful thoughts, lusts and wrong desires. The Lord is looking for people He can trust; He is looking for friends:

> "You are my friends if you do what I command you. No longer do I call you servants, for the servant does not know what his master is doing; but I have called you friends, for all that I have heard from my Father I have made known to you." (John 15:14-15).

Are you satisfied with just being His servant, or do you want to become His "friend?"

When we put His kingdom first in everything, there will be light, illumination, revelation released to us:

> "Light rises in the darkness for the upright…."
> (Psalm 112:4).

> "But the path of the righteous is like the light of dawn, which shines brighter and brighter until full day."
> (Proverbs 4:18).

As we are intent in doing God's will, not only will there be a supply of light and revelation given to us, but there will be an increase; our path will shine "brighter and brighter!"

Jesus said,

> "I Am the light of the world; he who follows me will not walk in darkness, but will have the light of life"
> (John 8:12).

As long as we follow Jesus, we will not walk in darkness, but there will be light released to us.

We are living in times that the Holy Spirit is looking for surrendered vessels, docile and obedient to His voice. To such He will empower and shower with revelation to carry out great exploits. In Luke 10:17, when the disciples returned from their mission full of joy and excitement because they "saw" that they could exercise authority over the enemy, Jesus said,

> "...blessed are the eyes which see what you see! For I tell you, that many prophets and kings desired to see what you see, and did not see it...." (Luke 10:23).

NEEDED: DISCERNMENT OF SPIRITS!

> "Woe to you, scribes and Pharisees, hypocrites! For you are like whitewashed tombs, which outwardly appear beautiful, but within they are full of dead men's bones and all uncleanness. So you also outwardly appear righteous to men, but within you are full of hypocrisy and iniquity." (Matthew 23:27-28).

The gift of discernment of spirits (1 Corinthians 12:10) will become more and more necessary in the days ahead. This gift of revelation enables us to "see" what spirit is motivating a person; we will be able to "see" the evil one at work trying to influence and control a certain situation. We will have a "behind the scenes" look at what is really happening in the spirit realm, so that we can act accordingly. No matter how dark the days become, as believers we will still have light:

> "...I will turn the darkness before them into light...."
> (Isaiah 42:16).

Remember what Jesus said,

> "I am the light of the world; he who follows Me will not walk in darkness, but will have the light of life."
> (John 8:12).

Just the fact that over 50% of Catholics put into the White House a president that is radically pro-abortion, indicates that we as Church are not walking in revelation nor discerning properly! This is tragic indeed, because as God's people gifted with the Holy Spirit (Who is the Spirit of truth), we have been empowered to "see" the truth in every situation. We don't know who we are! We don't know what our function as "church" is! We are supposed to be representing and expanding the kingdom of God on earth! We are supposed to be enforcing the victory and triumph of the Cross over every situation that is controlled by the enemy!

When we put our agendas ahead of God's, our vision becomes cloudy. Brothers and sisters, we must "seek His kingdom first" in everything! We must love truth and stand up for it! If we desire truth, we will find it. Jesus said,

> "Everyone who is of the truth hears my voice." (John 18:37).

> "When the Spirit of truth comes, he will guide you into all truth...." (John 16:12).

Out of love for truth and love for people this gift of discernment operates. It's meant to be used at all times: when praying for the captives to set them free; when making a decision so that we can make the one that pleases God; when listening to others so that we can "flow" in revelation; when voting for a President so that we elect the one that God desires!

The opposite is true: when we insist on having our "idols" and on doing things our own way, we become stubborn, stiff-necked , unteachable; God Himself will shut our eyes! Isaiah says,

> "They know not, nor do they discern; for he has shut their eyes, so that they cannot see, and their minds, so that they cannot understand." (Isaiah 44:18).

Other Bible translations say,

> "The idols have neither knowledge nor reason; their eyes

are coated so that they cannot see, and their hearts so that they cannot understand." (NAB).

"They know nothing, they understand nothing, since their eyes are incapable of seeing and their hearts of reflecting." (NJB).

This is a terrible situation to be in! According to the Scriptures, there comes a point that the Lord Himself blinds us! Could this happen to us today? Could we possibly miss what the Holy Spirit is doing today because of our stubbornness and rigidity?

Speaking of the Jews, the Apostle John says,

"Therefore they could not believe ... He has blinded their eyes and hardened their hearts...." (John 12:39-40).

In John 9, even after the Pharisees had witnessed the healing of a man blind from birth, they refused to believe that Jesus was the Messiah. They kicked out of the synagogue the man on whom Jesus had performed the miracle! Some even said that he was demonized and insane! (John 10:20). They rejected truth and Jesus told them,

"If you were blind, you would have no guilt; but now that you say, We see, your guilt remains." (John 9:41).

Could it be that many are suffering from a "spirit of stupor" (Romans 11:7) and a hardening of our hearts because we have

"...exchanged the truth about God for a lie and worshiped and served the creature rather than the Creator?" (Romans 1:23).

We have to love truth and hold on to it:

"Buy truth, and do not sell it...." (Proverbs 23:23).

Jesus, Truth incarnate, flowed in this gift of discernment as

He "saw" the real motivation behind the Pharisees and religious establishment of His day. These people didn't want truth; their desire was to remain in control and they rejected Him! Jesus "wept" because of their stubbornness and hardness of heart:

> "And when he drew near and saw the city he wept over it, saying 'Would that even today you knew the things that make for peace! But now they are hid from your eyes.'" (Luke 19:41-42).

We see Peter flowing in this gift as he properly discerned that Ananias was lying in Acts 5:1-11:

> "Ananias, why has satan filled your heart to lie to the Holy Spirit...."

In Acts 8:23, Peter told Simon, a magician with wrong motives,

> "For I see that you are in the gall of bitterness and in the bond of iniquity."

The Holy Spirit showed Peter the magician's heart.

The Apostle Paul, in his first missionary trip, encountered a false prophet who was trying to block the ministry:

> "But Saul, who is also called Paul, filled with the Holy Spirit, looked intently at him and said, You son of the devil, you enemy of all righteousness, full of all deceit and villainy...." (Acts 13:9-10).

As Paul "looked" at the man, the Holy Spirit downloaded revelation.

In Philippi, Acts 16, the Apostle Paul properly discerned the source motivating the girl that followed Silas and him for many days saying,

> "These men are servants of the Most High God, who proclaim to you the way of salvation" (v.17).

What this girl was saying was correct, but Paul discerned the source and realized it was demonic. Paul then casted out that evil spirit from the girl and set her free.

Brothers and sisters, we need to grow in this gift!

I have a dear friend in Tanzania whom I admire and respect. Last year I received a very warm and nice email from him; in the email he was asking me for help. He said that he was in another country (Nigeria) preaching, and was mugged and left with nothing. He was asking me for financial help. The email stated where to send the money directly. As I read and re-read the email, something didn't seem right. Because I am his friend and sister in the Lord, I was ready to send him the money; but there was "something" uneasy about his request in the pit of my stomach. Thank God for the gift of discernment! As I asked the Lord for more discernment, the Lord showed me that someone had stolen all his information, and this person, pretending to be my friend, was the one asking for the money. By the grace of God, I didn't send any money; my discernment was 100% accurate! Thank You, Holy Spirit! Later that year when I saw him, he told me that many of his friends had sent the money, believing it was him!

In the days ahead we need to properly discern what is going on because the enemy is an imitator, counterfeiter and loves confusion. Jesus said to His disciples:

> "And then if any one says to you, Look, here is the Christ! Or Look, there he is! Do not believe it. False Christs and false prophets will arise and show signs and wonders, to lead astray, if possible, the elect." (Mark 13:21-22).

Brothers and sisters, it's all about Jesus! If Jesus is being glorified, exalted, given the highest honor as the Son of God and only Savior of the world, the Holy Spirit is there. There are many good-sounding philosophies that talk about Jesus as a healer and prophet, but not as the only Savior of the world! Don't believe all the beautiful sounding philosophies that come before your eyes just because it sounds good! Check if Jesus is receiving all the glory and honor. Look at what John says:

"Beloved, do not believe every spirit, but test the spirits to see whether they are of God; for many false prophets have gone out into the world. By this you know the Spirit of God: every spirit which confesses that Jesus Christ has come in the flesh is of God, and every spirit which does not confess Jesus is not of God. This is the spirit of antichrist…." (1 John 4:1-3).

I say it's time to sharpen the gift of discernment of spirits!

GROWING IN THE FEAR OF THE LORD

"The fear of the Lord is the beginning of knowledge; fools despise wisdom and instruction." (Proverbs 1:7).

Without a healthy fear of the Lord there will be no real spiritual growth! We will remain stunted spiritually, like self-centered, immature children who think only about themselves. We will remain spiritually "blind" to the plans and purposes of the Lord and will not be able to make the right choices and move forward. Why would the Lord trust us with more, when we can't stand up to truth in the face of evil? True wisdom and knowledge is to hate what He hates and love what He loves!

"The fear of the Lord is hatred of evil…." (Proverbs 8:13).

"The fear of the Lord is a fountain of life, that one may avoid the snares of death." (Proverbs 14:27)

To fear the Lord is to be in awe of Him; to put Him first in everything as He deserves, even when it seems to be at our disadvantage! To fear the Lord is to make His priorities our priorities!

The early church in the Book of Acts moved in tremendous power; they also "feared the Lord!"

The religious authorities commanded Peter and John

"not to speak or teach at all in the name of Jesus." (Acts 4:18).

Peter and John answered:

> "Whether it is right in the sight of God to listen to you rather than to God, you must judge; for we cannot but speak of what we have seen and heard." (Acts 4:19-20).

Again, in Acts 5:28, they were told:

> "We strictly charged you not to teach in this name, yet here you have filled Jerusalem with your teaching...."

Peter and the apostles answered:

> "We must obey God rather than men." (Acts 5:29).

That believers today would desire to fill the earth with the Lord's teaching...!

That same demon that tried to stop the name of Jesus from being used then is still alive today! Haven't you heard it said, "Don't mention the name of Jesus; we don't want to offend anyone?" I was in a certain nation, ready to visit a refugee camp with the good news of the Gospel, when the priest in charge of the camp warned me not to use the name of Jesus; they didn't want the few Moslems in the refugee camp to be offended!

Paul writes:

> "...let us cleanse ourselves from every defilement of body and spirit, and make holiness perfect in the fear of God." (2 Corinthians 7:1).

Because our eyes are a gate through which defilement and filth can enter, we need to take authority of this gate and instead use it to grow in holiness and fear of the Lord. We want to keep a clean house!

It is the person who "fears" Him, that gets "taught" by the Lord:

> "Who is the man that fears the Lord? Him will he instruct

in the way that he should choose." (Psalm 25:12).

It is to the person who "fears" Him that becomes a friend of God:

> "The friendship of the Lord is for those who fear him...." (Psalm 25:14).

It is the person who "fears" Him that receives revelation of His covenant:

> "...and he makes known to them his covenant." (Psalm 25:14).

The person who walks in the fear of the Lord will be satisfied, protected and taken care of:

> "He fulfills the desire of all who fear him, he also hears their cry, and saves them." (Psalm 145:19).

> "O how abundant is thy goodness, which thou hast laid up for those who fear thee...in the covert of thy presence thou hidest them from the plots of men; thou holdest them safe under thy shelter from the strife of tongues." (Psalm 31:19-20).

I like the story of the midwives in Exodus 1. Pharaoh, who is a type of satan, commanded the midwives to kill all the Hebrew baby boys, because God's people were growing very fast. This was a satanic attack against God's people; the enemy trying to destroy them because he knew that a deliverer would come from this people. Pharaoh told the midwives,

> "When you serve as midwife to the Hebrew women, and see them upon the birthstool, if it is a son, you shall kill him; but if it is a daughter, she shall live." (Exodus 1:16).

The midwives feared God and did not do as Pharaoh requested. This took a lot of guts! Thank God these midwives were not into "political correctness!" They had the correct perspective and stood firm in their beliefs; God was God and Pharaoh was not.

> "But the midwives feared God, and did not do as the king of Egypt commanded them, but let the male children live. So the king of Egypt called the midwives, and said to them, Why have you done this, and let the male children live? The midwives said to Pharaoh, Because the Hebrew women are not like Egyptian women; for they are vigorous and are delivered before the midwife comes to them." (Exodus 1:17-19).

Because the midwives feared God,

> "God dealt well with the midwives; and the people multiplied and grew very strong. And because the midwives feared God he gave them families." (Exodus 1:20-21).

Two women stood up for God and not only God blessed them for it, but their decision to uphold God first had great effects on the rest of the people: the people multiplied and grew very strong!

> "For as the heavens are high above the earth, so great is his steadfast love toward those who fear him...." (Psalm 103:11).

I WANT TO SEE JESUS!

> "And even if our gospel is veiled, it is veiled only to those who are perishing. In their case the god of this world has blinded the minds of the unbelievers, to keep them from seeing the light of the gospel of the glory of Christ, who is the likeness of God." (2 Corinthians 4:3-4).

One of the functions of the enemy is to blind us from the truth. Who is THE TRUTH? JESUS! The enemy places a "spiritual veil" over our eyes so that we can't see "the light of the gospel of the glory of Christ...." Veils of pride, rebellion and self-sufficiency keep us blinded from our need for Jesus. Sometimes even veils of "religion" can keep us from encountering the real thing! I remember when my sister shared the gospel with me and talked about Jesus; I thought she was crazy and had lost her mind. I could not understand what was "wrong" with her. After all, every year I would win the religion award in school! I knew my answers very well to the questions asked; but the reality was that I was lost, blind and deaf. After praying for me for seven years with her friends, finally, I "saw" my need for Jesus. I share this testimony for two reasons: all of us have people in our lives that still need to have an encounter with Jesus; realize that they are "blind" spiritually and need to have their veils removed. They need to SEE! Ask the Holy Spirit, our wonderful Helper, to reveal to you how to pray for that person. The other reason is that a person can be baptized and confirmed, have gone to Catholic school, married in Church, and still be BLIND! That was me! I believe the Church is packed with people like that; they go through the motions, they "do" the "right thing" by coming to Church, but still they have not had an encounter with the Lord. They have not experienced repentance, conversion, nor the transforming power of the Holy Spirit. Their lives don't change; they are spiritually fruitless with no spiritual vision for their lives.

Paul says in 1Corinthians 12:3, "...and no one can say Jesus is Lord except by the Holy Spirit."

It takes a "seeing" to know that Jesus is Lord and Savior. It's the function of the Holy Spirit to reveal and exalt Jesus. As temples of the Holy Spirit, we have been empowered and anointed to point and lead people to Jesus. We have what the world needs: JESUS!

Not only are we to go out and proclaim the Good News, but the Lord will bring people to us with this desire: to see Jesus. It happened to Phillip in John 12:20-22,

"Sir, we wish to see Jesus."

How do we make this invisible God visible? Our helper, the Holy Spirit, the Spirit of Truth, will help us as we give testimony and share the Gospel by confirming our message with signs following (Mark 16:20). The Holy Spirit will work alongside us and will release conviction on those who hear (John 16:7-11), just like it happened to Peter in the house of Cornelius as he preached to the Gentiles (Acts 10:44). Jesus must be known personally as Savior and Lord, for this is necessary for our salvation. The Apostle Paul says in Romans 10:9 that

> "...if you confess with your lips that Jesus is Lord and believe in your heart that God raised him from the dead, you will be saved."

Jesus is the only Savior! We cannot save ourselves nor can any one else save us! On that Cross the Son of God died and shed His blood for you and me so that our sins could be wiped away! In this fact we place our trust for our salvation and we "confess" this truth with our tongue.

Even to "see" the kingdom of God a person needs to be born again. Jesus told Nicodemus,

> "Truly, truly, I say to you, unless one is born anew, he cannot see the kingdom of God." (John 3:5).

And there is much more revelation about the Lord! There are different aspects of His nature and character that He wants to reveal to us so that we can walk in victory in this planet. At the Cross He bought an inheritance for us at the price of His life so that we could experience the "abundant life" (John 10:10): healing, deliverance, wholeness; He wants total restoration of our lives, spirit, soul and body! So it's good for us to know Jesus our Healer, Jesus the Good Shepherd, Jesus our Bridegroom, Jesus the Lord of Hosts, Jesus our Provider, Jesus our Peace, Jesus our Righteousness, for example. As we follow Jesus and have our minds renewed by the Word of God, there is unfolding revelation of Who He is! Every time we have a difficulty and we trust Him, He will reveal Himself in the way we need so that we experience His overcoming power and the extension of His Kingdom in us and through us.

Joshua, Moses' successor and the one leading God's people to take over the Promised Land, had an amazing encounter with the Lord of Hosts before attacking Jericho. He needed this "new" revelation of the Lord because now they were on the offensive, kicking out the enemy out of the Promised Land in order to possess it. Jericho was a well protected and highly fortified city. It was a strong fortress with thick walls surrounding the city. I've read somewhere that Jericho's walls were so thick, that chariot races could be held on top of the walls!

In Joshua 5, we find Joshua by Jericho; he might have been thinking about what strategy the Lord had in mind for them to take over Jericho, because humanly speaking, it was just an impossible situation. There was no way that they could come against this fortress on their own strength, and Joshua might have been pondering the situation. Something happened when Joshua "lifted up his eyes!"

> "When Joshua was by Jericho, he lifted up his eyes and looked and behold, a man stood before him with his drawn sword in his hand; and Joshua went to him and said to him, 'Are you for us, or for our adversaries?' And he said, 'No; but as commander of the army of the Lord I have now come.' And Joshua fell on his face to the earth, and worshiped...." (Joshua 5:13-14).

What a comfort for Joshua to know that the Lord had come to lead God's army into battle; that meant victory! I believe that today we need revelation of the commander of the army of the Lord! He is the Lord of Hosts, the commander of the heavenly armies Who fights on our behalf. As we put His Kingdom first and do His will, He has angels at His disposal to carry out His plans of victory!

In the Book of Revelation chapter 19 we see Jesus coming back as a warrior:

> "From His mouth issues a sharp sword with which to smite the nations, and he will rule them with a rod of iron; he will tread the wine press of the fury of the wrath of

> God the Almighty. On his robe and on his thigh he has a name inscribed, King of kings and Lord of lords."

We need to "see" Jesus as the Lord of Hosts; we need to see Him as the "man of war" (Exodus 15:3). Darker days are ahead for this nation, and like Joshua, we need this revelation to battle the enemy and enforce the victory of Calvary in every area where the enemy is in control! We need to take back and possess what the enemy has stolen from us! Think of our families, our children, our cities, our schools, our government, the mass media, the entertainment business, etc. Think of the Church! Think of the innocent blood shed in this country because of abortions! I think it's time for WAR! Lift up your eyes and "see" that you are not alone; the Lord of Hosts is for you and not against you! I don't care how thick those "walls" are; with the Lord on your side you are in the winning team!

Another revelation we need to receive is that of the Lord being our provider. There is no lack in His kingdom! As a matter of fact, He has already provided everything that we need in this life. The Apostle Paul says,

> "And my God will supply every need of yours according to his riches in glory in Christ Jesus." (Philippians 4:19).

God's supply is according to his riches in glory! No limits! It's important to "see" this truth because we are the ones that constantly place limitations and restrictions on what God can and can't provide! We limit His power when we are not in faith, because "without faith it is impossible to please God." (Hebrews 11:6).

In Romans 8:32, the Apostle Paul says,

> "He who did not spare his own Son but gave him up for us all, will he not also give us all things with him?"

"All things" come attached with the greatest gift of all: JESUS! We need to "see" this truth so that we don't go through life like hopeless, abandoned orphans who have no helper and no provision!

Abraham was about to sacrifice his son Isaac when the angel of the Lord prevented him from doing so; he "lifted up his eyes" and caught vision of the provision:

> "And Abraham lifted up his eyes and looked, and behold, behind him was a ram, caught in a thicket by his horns; and Abraham went and took the ram, and offered it up as a burnt offering instead of his son. So Abraham called the name of that place The Lord will provide...."
> (Genesis 22:13-14).

Just like the Lord provided a ram for Abraham, He has provided a Savior for the human race and He has given us the Holy Spirit to live out the new life. Do you "see" it? Whatever need we have, it has been provided in Christ Jesus! We have been blessed with the "blessing of Abraham" (Galatians 3:13) whom God "blessed in all things" (Genesis 24:1). There is no lack in the Kingdom! Lift up your eyes to God's provision and receive by faith what you need:

> "...those who seek the Lord lack no good thing."
> (Psalm 34:10).

As we seek His kingdom first, the Lord provides for everything that is needed; His supply is always flowing for those who are His. 2 Chronicles 16:9 says,

> "For the eyes of the Lord run to and fro throughout the whole earth, to show his might in behalf of those whose heart is blameless toward him."

Jesus describes Himself as the Good Shepherd (John 10:11-14). Like David, we can say with confidence

> "The Lord is my shepherd, I shall not want..."
> (Psalm 23:1).

For some reason, Psalm 23 is always read in funerals! This revelation is for now, as we journey on planet earth! It's comforting to know that we shall lack nothing (spirit, soul and body) as the Lord Jesus shepherds us. Look how He takes care of us:

He provides (v.1).

He gives us rest, refreshing, restoration (v.2).

He leads us (v.3).

He walks us "through" the dark moments so that we don't get stuck (v.4)

He protects us (v.4).

He blesses in front of our enemies; and to overflowing! (v.5).

He anoints us (v.5).

Verse 6 is very powerful:

"Surely goodness and mercy shall follow me all the days of my life...."

You must "see" yourself followed by God's goodness and mercy, not by crisis and disaster!

In John 10:27-28, Jesus says,

"My sheep hear my voice, and I know them, and they follow me; and I give them eternal life, and they shall never perish, and no one shall snatch them out of my hand."

Whatever you are going through, "lift up your eyes" to the Good Shepherd and allow Him to shepherd you! Experience the security that comes from belonging to Him! You are in His hand; it's the only firm, solid, stable, place there is. Look at what the Lord says in Ezekiel 34:15-16:

"I myself will be the shepherd of my sheep, and I will make them lie down, says the Lord God. I will seek the

> lost, and I will bring back the strayed, and I will bind up the crippled, and I will strengthen the weak…."

Get to know the heart of the Shepherd! Spend time with Him and "see" His goodness and kindness!

If you are restless, let Him give you rest!

If you are lost, let Him find you!

If you are hurt, let Him heal you!

If you are weak, let Him strengthen you!

As Rebekah approached her future home to meet her future husband, she "lifted up her eyes" and saw Isaac:

> "And Rebekah lifted up her eyes, and when she saw Isaac, she alighted from the camel, and said to the servant, Who is the man yonder, walking in the field to meet us?" The servant said, It is my master." (Genesis 24:64-65).

Rebekah is a picture of the Bride of Christ; she had journeyed through a difficult, long road. She trusted Eliezer, Abraham's servant, who is a type of the Holy Spirit, to take her to meet her future spouse. Eliezer knew the way, and Rebekah totally trusted him to take her to the right place. In the same way, we must trust the Holy Spirit in our journey to meet Jesus our Bridegroom. It takes a revelation, a "lifting up" of our eyes, to see and experience the love of Jesus, our Bridegroom! Expect visitations of your bridegroom as you journey to see Him face to face!

> "O that you would kiss me with the kisses of your mouth! For your love is better than wine,
> Your anointing oils are fragrant, your name is oil poured out; therefore the maidens love you.
> Draw me after you, let us make haste. The king has brought me into his chambers.
> We will exult and rejoice in you; we will extol your love more than wine; rightly do they love you."
> (Song of Solomon 1:2-4).

The Lord wants a glorious bride, one "without spot or wrinkle or any such thing, that she might be holy and without blemish." (Ephesians 5:27). Revelation of Jesus as our Bridegroom will help us stay faithful to Him and not become a friend of the world! (James 4:4). Once we experience the fire of His love nothing else matters! Nothing compares to Him! We will desire to spend time with Him because it becomes our joy to do so! When He becomes our treasure then we know that He has captured our hearts! He is a faithful Bridegroom Who will not abandon nor reject us! By faith, lift up your eyes to your Bridegroom King and ask the Holy Spirit to start revealing to you the beauty of Jesus!

How awesome when we receive revelation of Jesus our healer! The first revelation of Himself that the Lord gave His people after they crossed the Red Sea, was that of Him being a healer:

> "...I am the Lord, your healer." (Exodus 15:26).

On the Cross He took every sickness and every disease so that we could be healed (Isaiah 53:4-5); healing is our inheritance! Are you sick, in pain, depressed? Lift up your eyes to Jesus your healer and by faith receive your healing! Your healing already took place in the Cross over 2,000 years ago! "By His wounds you were healed" (1Peter 2:24). Psalm 103:2-3 says,

> "Bless the Lord, O my soul, and forget not all his benefits,
> Who forgives all your iniquity, who heals all your
> diseases...."

Are there benefits for God's people? You bet! Healing is one of them! He has provided healing for our entire being: spirit, soul and body! As we meditate on the Gospels, we see that Jesus spent much time healing the sick; he never turned anyone away that came asking for healing! Not only that, He has commissioned us to heal the sick! (Matthew 10:7-8; Mark 16:18). This is a manifestation of the power of the Gospel! (1 Corinthians 4:20).

Another revelation of Jesus that we need to embrace is Jesus, the Prince of Peace. The whole world is seeking peace; people in the world are restless, anxious, stressed out, fearful and upset.

They need to take sleeping pills in order to sleep at night, or go to Happy Hour in the local bar to forget their misery. The truth is that there is peace only in Jesus Christ. He has made peace for us with the Father through His blood:

> "...and through him to reconcile to himself all things, whether on earth or in heaven, making peace by the blood of his cross (Colossians 1:20).

No amount of money, no amount of good works, no amount of houses, pills, cars and material objects can obtain peace with God: only the blood of Jesus, as we repent and turn to the One that loved us enough to die for us! Right now, in the presence of the Lord, humble yourself and acknowledge that Jesus is your peace! Receive the peace that only He can give and thank Him for it! Paul prayed:

> "Now may the Lord of peace himself give you peace at all times in all ways." (2 Thessalonians 3:16).

No matter what we are going through, we can actually remain in peace when the Prince of Peace lives in us; even in airplanes in turbulent weather!

Jesus said,

> "Peace I leave with you; my peace I give to you; not as the world gives do I give to you. Let not your hearts be troubled, neither let them be afraid." (John 14:27).

The Lord doesn't want us to be troubled nor fearful. He has provided the way to live in perfect peace in this planet:

> "Thou dost keep him in perfect peace, whose mind is stayed on thee, because he trusts in thee." (Isaiah 26:3).

Trusting in the Lord releases perfect peace. It's in this place of quiet and rest that we operate and are positioned to receive revelation from the Lord to carry on with the works of Jesus. The enemy wants to keep us "busy" in the land of distraction with striving, fear, worry, anxiety. It's hard to hear and see in the Spirit when we are bound by these things.

This lifestyle of peace and rest in the Lord is available for you. Can you "see" it? What are you anxious and worried about? Get into the Word of God and search the Scriptures for the promises that pertain to your situation. Renew your mind with the truth of the Word of God and start trusting Him in that place of fear, worry and anxiety, which are not from the Lord.

Paul says in Philippians 4:6-7,

> "Have no anxiety about anything, but in everything by prayer and supplication with thanksgiving let your requests be made known to God. And the peace of God, which surpasses all understanding, will keep your hearts and your minds in Christ Jesus."

In prayer we give our burdens to the Lord and the peace of God will guard our hearts and minds. There is a transaction that should take place when we meet the Lord in prayer: we give Him all our burdens and He gives us His peace as we wait for the breakthrough. This peace is actually a weapon against the enemy. Paul says in Romans 16:20,

> "...the God of peace will soon crush satan under your feet."

When we walk in peace we crush satan under our feet! Don't leave that place of peace; it's not only your inheritance but also your protection!

Another revelation of Jesus that will help us remain steadfast is the fact that Jesus is our righteousness. We can rest in this fact! Paul says in Romans 3:21-24,

> "But now the righteousness of God has been manifested apart from law, although the law and the prophets bear witness to it, the righteousness of God through faith in Jesus Christ for all who believe. For there is no distinc-

tion; since all have sinned and fall short of the glory of God, they are justified by his grace as a gift, through the redemption which is in Christ Jesus…."

Our righteousness is a gift from God! Thank You, Jesus! It is not by keeping the law, because we are unable on our own strength to fulfill its demands; it is "apart from the law," through faith in Christ Jesus! It's impossible for us to become "holy" through our own strength and effort! That's why Jesus had to come and save us. Embrace His grace! The Apostle Paul had been an "excellent" Pharisee, always striving to do everything right on his own strength; but when he met Jesus Christ he realized that righteousness was something he could not earn according to his own efforts. Paul's heart was broken for his own people, because they refused to believe the righteousness that came through faith in Christ Jesus:

> "…I have great sorrow and unceasing anguish in my heart. For I could wish that I myself were accursed and cut off from Christ for the sake of my brethren, my kinsmen by race." (9:2-3).

> "For being ignorant of the righteousness that comes from God, and seeking to establish their own, they did not submit to God's righteousness." (Romans 10:3).

Are you still trying to establish your own righteousness? We can't operate out of our righteousness; as Isaiah says,

> "We have all become like one who is unclean, and all our righteous deeds are like a polluted garment."
> (Isaiah 64:6).

Our own righteousness is like filthy rags from God's perspective. In Christ Jesus we have become "the righteousness of God." (2 Corinthians 5:21). We walk by faith, trusting in the Lord that His Word is true!

"And to one who does not work but trusts him who justifies the ungodly, his faith is reckoned as righteousness." (Romans 4:5).

Lift up your eyes to the Lord and realize that He freely gives you his righteousness! Repent from trying and striving to achieve it on your own. You don't have to work for it. This results in great peace and freedom from the enemy, who loves to accuse us of everything that has been wiped away by the blood of Jesus! We are born again (1 Peter 1:23); we are a new creation (2 Corinthians 5:17); we have been transferred out of darkness into God's kingdom (Colossians 1:13) and empowered to walk in newness of life (Romans 6:4). We are citizens of God's kingdom (Ephesians 2:19) and we have been clothed with His righteousness (Isaiah 62:10). If we don't "see" this truth, the enemy will have a great time tormenting us, reminding us of all our failures and keeping us in bondage through the shame, the memories of past failures, self-pity, self-hatred, etc.

The Apostle Paul wrote in Philippians 3:7-9,

"Indeed I count everything as loss because of the surpassing worth of knowing Christ Jesus my Lord. For his sake I have suffered the loss of all things, and count them as refuse, in order that I may gain Christ and be found in him, not having a righteousness of my own, based on law, but that which is through faith in Christ, the righteousness from God that depends on faith...."

It's a matter of humbling ourselves before our God, repenting, believing and receiving like children what the Lord freely offers to us! Admit your helplessness and receive His righteousness!

"Behold, the days are coming, says the Lord, when I will raise up for David a righteous Branch, and he shall reign as king and deal wisely, and shall execute justice and righteousness in the land. In his days Judah will be saved, and Israel will dwell securely. And this is the name by which he will be called: The Lord is our righteousness!" (Jeremiah 23:5-6).

"JESUS LIFTED UP HIS EYES ALSO!"

> "Jesus said to them, "Truly, truly, I say to you, the Son can do nothing of his own accord, but only what he sees the Father doing; for whatever he does, that the Son does likewise. For the Father loves the Son, and shows him all that he himself is doing…." (John 5:19-20).

Out of the love relationship Jesus had with His Father flowed the revelation Jesus needed to release the kingdom. It is the same for you and me! How much do you want the Holy Spirit's help in your life? It will flow out of your love relationship with Jesus; if you love Him you will obey Him. Obeying Him becomes a joy! Jesus said in John 14:21,

> "He who has my commandments and keeps them, he it is who loves me; and he who loves me will be loved by my Father, and I will love him and manifest myself to him."

As you set out to put His kingdom first, Jesus will reveal or manifest to you what you need in order to extend His kingdom on earth. He is the vine, we are the branches; it's the branches that bear the fruit of this relationship with the Lord. Apart from Him we can do nothing! (Jesus 15:5). Why do we need to remain abiding in the Vine? Because we cannot do anything on our own! The works of the flesh (not initiated by the Holy Spirit) will not produce good fruit. We want to flow in the Spirit, just like Jesus, so that He be glorified and His kingdom extended on earth as it is in heaven through you and through me!

In Matthew 14:14-21 Jesus encountered an impossible situation: feeding a crowd of 5,000 men (not including women and children) with only 5 loaves of bread and 2 fish. What did Jesus do? In verse 19 we see the key to the success of His ministry:

> "…he looked up to heaven…."

Jesus didn't freak out, he didn't hold a board meeting to formulate a plan, but He turned to His Father for the strategy. In

John's gospel, John 6:5-14, the first thing Jesus did when He saw the crowd approaching was to lift up His eyes:

> "Lifting up His eyes, then, and seeing that a multitude was coming to him, Jesus said to Phillip, 'How are we to buy bread, so that these people may eat?' This He said to test him, for He himself knew what He would do."

How did Jesus know beforehand what He would do? HE LOOKED UP TO HEAVEN! He looked not to the natural, but to the invisible, supernatural realm to receive a download from the Father. This was a pattern in the ministry of Jesus.

In Mark 7:32-37, a deaf man with a speech problem was brought to Jesus. Jesus did several things:

Took him aside

Put his fingers into his ears

Spat and touched his tongue

LOOKED UP TO HEAVEN

Sighed and spoke a command for the ears to open.

What was the result? "And his ears were opened, his tongue was released, and he spoke plainly."

In John 11, the resurrection of Lazarus, Jesus "lifted up his eyes" (v.41) after the stone had been removed; after that He just flowed in thanksgiving and shouted to Lazarus to come out. The result: a resurrection! We see that in everything that Jesus did, He was connected to His Father.

John 17 is one of the most beautiful and touching Scriptures in the whole Bible. This is the prayer of Jesus to His Father just before the passion. It reveals God's heart for the unity of His people. Before speaking Jesus "lifted up his eyes to heaven and said...." (John 17:1). Even to pray, Jesus first connected to His Father! Is it possible to live this way? With the help of the Holy Spirit we can! The Holy Spirit "searches everything, even the depths of God." (1 Corinthians 2:10). The Holy Spirit will help us search the heart of God for every situation we encounter. The real question is: whose will do we want? Ours or His?

Jesus used His eyes effectively because His food was to do His Father's will and accomplish his work (John 4:34). As He went He saw in the Spirit realm and acted accordingly. He said,

> "Truly, truly, I say to you, the Son can do nothing of his own accord, but only what he sees the Father doing; for whatever he does, that the Son does likewise."
> (John 5:19).

Jesus called forth His disciples from ordinary people that He came across. Always connected to His Father, He would receive a download of revelation as to what the Father wanted. He was able to see the hidden treasure in people's hearts:

> "And passing along by the Sea of Galilee, he saw Simon and Andrew the brother of Simon casting a net in the sea; for they were fishermen. And Jesus said to them, 'Follow me and I will make you become fishers of men.'"
> (Mark 1:16-17).

> "And going on a little farther, he saw James the son of Zebedee and John his brother, who were in their boat mending the nets. And immediately he called them...."
> (Mark 1:19-20).

> "As Jesus passed on from there, he saw a man called Matthew sitting at the tax office; and he said to him, 'Follow me.'" (Matthew 9:9).

> "He brought him up to Jesus. Jesus looked at him, and said, 'So you are Simon the son of John? You shall be called Cephas' (which means Peter)" (John 1:42).

> "Jesus saw Nathanael coming to Him, and said of him, 'Behold, an Israelite indeed, in whom is no guile!'"
> (John 1:47).

Jesus saw in every situation an opportunity to extend the kingdom:

> "Seeing the crowds, he went up on the mountain, and when he sat down his disciples came to him. And he opened his mouth and taught them…." (Matthew 5:1-2).

> "As he went ashore he saw a great throng; and he had compassion on them, and healed their sick." (Matthew 14:14).

> "As he landed he saw a great throng, and he had compassion on them, because they were like sheep without a shepherd; and he began to teach them many things." (Mark 6:34).

> "Lifting up His eyes, then, and seeing that a multitude was coming to him, Jesus said to Philip, 'How are we to buy bread, so that these people may eat?'" (John 6:5).

> "When Jesus saw him and knew that he had been lying there a long time, he said to him, 'Do you want to be healed?'" (John 5:6).

> "And when Jesus saw her, he called her and said to her, 'Woman, you are freed from your infirmity.'"
> (Luke 13:12).

> "And when the Lord saw her, he had compassion on her and said to her, 'Do not weep.' And he came and touched the bier, and the bearers stood still. And he said, 'Young man, I say to you, arise.'" (Luke 7:13-14).

Even from the Cross, in the midst of great pain and suffering, Jesus was using His eyes to carry out God's plans:

> "When Jesus saw his mother, and the disciple who he loved standing near, he said to his mother, 'Woman, behold, your son!' Then he said to the disciple, 'Behold, your mother!'" (John 19:26).

I believe that God is looking for surrendered vessels that He can use powerfully to extend His kingdom on earth as it is in heaven. Accomplishing His will needs to become our food! He is waiting for our YES! We have been gifted and empowered to walk like Jesus walked. Church, we must rid ourselves from the identity crisis that we have been suffering from! We are not "poor, little orphans" with no hope and no future. We are sons and daughters of the Most High God with a great future ahead of us if we just wake up! The Apostle Paul says,

> "For the creation waits with eager longing for the revealing of the sons of God." (Romans 8:19).

It seems that even creation knows that the sons of God are the ones that have been anointed and empowered to make wrong things right!

NO MORE SCALES!

> "And immediately something like scales fell from his eyes and he regained his sight." (Acts 9:18).

This is the Apostle Paul's testimony after his encounter with the Lord, when he was left blinded by "a light from heaven, brighter than the sun..." (Acts 26:13). The disciple Ananias laid hands on him to be filled with the Holy Spirit and Paul regained his sight. For the first time in his life Paul started to see as God sees when the scales fell from his eyes. Previously, Paul had been a religious zealot who thought he was following God and doing His will, until he had an encounter with the risen Lord. After Ananias prayed with him, the direction of Paul's life totally changed! He received God's vision for his life and was transformed from the greatest persecutor of the Church into a mighty evangelist, apostle, prophet, teacher and author. The Lord sent him to open eyes:

> "...I send you to open their eyes, that they may turn from darkness to light and from the power of Satan to God, that

> they may receive forgiveness of sins and a place among those who are sanctified by faith in me." (Acts 26:18).

Before a person can turn from darkness to light, from the power of satan to God in order to receive forgiveness of sins and sanctification, their eyes have to open! Just like Paul, we have been anointed to open people's eyes. We are a "light" for those in darkness in order to bring salvation to the lost. (Acts 13:47).

WE are called to

> "give light to those who sit in darkness and in the shadow of death...." (Luke 1:79).

We are not called to be "politically correct" but to be and give light to those in darkness! Jesus said,

> "You are the light of the world. A city set on a hill cannot be hid. Nor do men light a lamp and put it under a bushel, but on a stand, and it gives light to all in the house." (Matthew 5:14-15).

Do you realize that you are supposed to be a "lamp?" Have you found your "stand" from which you shine the light of Christ? Do you see the importance of guarding our eye gate, so that what we release is light and not darkness? Wherever the Lord has called you, there you are to be and give light to those around you. Just shine! How do we shine? As we abide in him and keep our eyes lifted up to the Lord, we will flow in the spirit and the light of Christ will automatically shine in and through us! We need to stay plugged to the spirit and we'll see people being drawn to the light.

Paul knew the importance of seeing from God's perspective; he knew the need to see in the Spirit realm. In Ephesians 1:17-19 he prayed

> "...that the God of our Lord Jesus Christ, the Father of glory, may give you a spirit of wisdom and of revelation in the knowledge of him, having the eyes of your hearts enlightened, that you may know what is the hope to

> which he has called you, what are the riches of his glorious inheritance in the saints, and what is the immeasurable greatness of his power in us who believe...."

We need revelation, we need our eyes enlightened so that we can see as God sees! How else can we partner with Him if we are not on the same page?

The Lord sent the prophet Samuel to Bethlehem to anoint the next king of Israel; He had had enough of Saul. Samuel was sent to the house of Jesse:

> "Fill your horn with oil, and go; I will send you to Jesse the Bethlehemite, for I have provided for myself a king among his sons." (1 Samuel 16:1).

Jesse prepared for the prophet's visit and gathered his sons together, except for one, David. Samuel came and looked at Jesse's sons and was very impressed with what he saw with his eyes. When he saw Eliab, Samuel thought,

> "Surely the Lord's anointed is before him." (v. 6).

Samuel saw in Eliab a future king; tall and handsome. He assumed that he was the chosen one, but God had somebody else in mind. I want you to "see" what the Lord told Samuel:

> "Do not look on his appearance or on the height of his stature, because I have rejected him; for the Lord sees not as man sees; man looks on the outward appearance, but the Lord looks at the heart." (v.7).

When will we ever understand that we cannot judge and make decisions on what we see with our physical eyes, but rather get into the Spirit realm for the revelation, wisdom and truth that we need? When will we allow the Holy Spirit to reveal to us what is hidden? We need to start looking at the heart, just like the Lord. The Scriptures clearly reveal that the instruments that God chooses confound the world's standards. Look at what the

Apostle Paul says in 1 Corinthians 1:26-29:

> "For consider your call, brethren; not many of you were wise according to worldly standards, not many were powerful, not many were of noble birth; but God chose what is foolish in the world to shame the wise, God chose what is weak in the world to shame the strong. God chose what is low and despised in the world, even things that are not, to bring to nothing things that are, so that no human being might boast in the presence of God."

We need our spiritual eyes to be opened so that we can see as God sees. Why could Jesus choose people like Peter, James, John, Matthew, etc.? Because He saw their hearts; He saw the "finished products!" The Apostles were uneducated, untrained simple folks. They were not learned nor sophisticated. The Lord doesn't call the qualified; He qualifies the called! We keep on doing the reverse!

Seven of Jesse's sons passed before Samuel and the Lord rejected all of them. They looked good and smelled good, but the Lord had not chosen any of them. Finally the prophet asked Jesse,

> "Are all your sons here? And he said, there remains yet the youngest, but behold, he is keeping the sheep." (v.11).

In Jesse's mind David didn't even qualify to meet the prophet personally; he was just good enough for taking care of the sheep. After all, he had seven other sons who seemed better prospects than David. Samuel asked for David to be brought in. When David showed up, the Lord said to Samuel,

> "Arise, anoint him; for this is he."

Last year in New Zealand I was ministering to a young man that had gone through a terrible past. He had a huge "father wound." His father had never affirmed him, rejected him and hit him every day. He was sent far away from home to boarding schools. He became rebellious and got involved in drugs, alcohol, sexual immorality. He was carrying a lot of shame, rejection and emotional pain. He had no peace, no joy and lots of pain in his back; he couldn't sleep at night. He needed much deliverance and inner healing. Once he forgave his father he started to experience peace. I knew that the Lord had big plans for him and wanted to use him to proclaim the good news and bring a huge harvest into the kingdom. On the last ministry, we prayed in tongues asking the Lord for a vision for his life. The Lord gave him a vision and in this vision he saw a man on a stage, preaching to many, many people. I knew that the man on the stage preaching was him, but my friend didn't realize it! I asked him, "Who is the man on the stage preaching? " He didn't know, so again we prayed in tongues asking the Lord to show him. Finally, I asked him again, "Who is the man on the stage preaching?" Weeping, he said "It's me; I just need to believe it."

It was difficult for my friend to believe that the Lord loved him and wanted to use him powerfully. All his life he had believed the lies of the enemy: "I am good for nothing;" "I am a failure;" "I am unlovable;" "I can't do anything right." Now, Papa was telling him the opposite! The scales came off and when I left he was weeping tears of joy and experiencing love in his heart for his father for the first time in his life!

Brothers and sisters, we need to see from God's perspective, we need to see with His eyes! The scales from our eyes must fall out so that we can see people prophetically and see what God wants to do in their lives!

I WANT DREAMS!

"And it shall come to pass afterward,
That I will pour out my spirit on all flesh;
Your sons and your daughters shall prophesy,
Your old men shall dream dreams,
And your young men shall see visions." (Joel 2:28)

This is what Peter quoted on the day of Pentecost when the Holy Spirit was poured out on the believers that were gathered in the upper room (Acts 2:17). Dreams and visions are part of our inheritance! These are some of the ways in which the Lord communicates with us. Throughout the Scriptures and in the history of God's people, dreams have been used powerfully by the Lord to reveal His plans and purposes for mankind. Remember, we are co-laborers with the Holy Spirit (2 Corinthians 6:1);

We are in partnership with the Holy Spirit to bring a lost world to Jesus, Who

> "desires all men to be saved and to come to the knowledge of the truth. For there is one God, and there is one mediator between God and men, the man Christ Jesus, who gave himself as a ransom for all…."
> (1 Timothy 2:3-6).

We need to start positioning ourselves in a place where the Lord can trust us with dreams and visions so that we can partner effectively with Him to extend His kingdom on earth and to bring the end time harvest of souls into His Kingdom. This involves seeing! It was the "seer" gifting that landed Joseph and Daniel in places of great authority. The Lord used them powerfully and everyone around them knew that the Lord was with them. The "kings" of the world needed what God had deposited in them! After Joseph interpreted Pharaoh's dream, Pharaoh told Joseph,

> "Since God has shown you all this, there is none so discreet and wise as you are; you shall be over my house, and all my people shall order themselves as you command; Only as regard the throne will I be greater than you."
> And Pharaoh said to Joseph, behold, I have set you over all the land of Egypt." (Genesis 41:39-41).

> "A man's gift makes room for him and brings him before great men." (Proverbs 18:16).

We, as God's people on earth, should be flowing with all the revelation/seer gifts that the Lord has given us in the Spirit. When we "see" the importance of seeing in the spirit realm and start functioning in those gifts, kings, rulers, princes of this world will come knocking on our doors because they will need what we have! And the Lord will be glorified! Isn't this what happened with Naaman and Elisha the prophet (2 Kings 5)? I think that we have been blind to this truth; we need and have a responsibility to develop the revelation/seer gifts for the sake of the human race and for the glory of God! After all, as Catholics we have been baptized as "prophets, kings and priests!" I say "It's time to develop, activate and use this anointing!"

Look at some of the ways that dreams were used by God to bring forth His plans:

> It was a dream that changed Joseph's mind about marrying Mary. (Matthew 1:20-21);
>
> It was a in a dream that Joseph was warned to leave Bethlehem in haste because of Herod's plan to kill the babies. (Matthew 2:13);
>
> It was a dream that the Lord used to warn the three wise men to use another route on their return. (Matthew 2:12);
>
> It was in a dream that the Lord told Joseph to go back to Nazareth. (Matthew 2:22);
>
> It was through dreams that the Lord revealed to Joseph his destiny. (Genesis 37:5-9);
>
> It was through a dream that the Lord warned Pilate's wife about Jesus. (Matthew 27:19).

In my own life the Lord has used dreams to communicate with me. For example, confirmation of going to Uganda to proclaim the Word of God came through a dream. In the dream I saw myself going "fishing" to Uganda with all the gear that I needed. In another dream I saw myself with another person in Uganda, the Lord showing me specifically whom I should take with me. Before the first WOW conference I had a very vivid dream in which

I was in labor, giving birth, and the mid-wife was my mother. These are just some examples of dreams in my life and how the Lord used them for confirmation, guidance, encouragement. Are all dreams from God? Of course not, but you need to discern the source and check for the fruit of the Spirit in the dream. The devil is in the business of "imitation," and because he is a thief he tries to give us dreams also! No need to fear, because the Holy Spirit is the Spirit of Truth and He will guide you into all truth. We cannot allow fear to control us!

During my last ministry in Uganda, I had a dream in which I was proclaiming the Word of God to a multitude and I was quoting from the Scriptures,

> "Salvation belongs to our God who sits upon the throne, and to the Lamb!" (Revelation 7:10).

I thank the Lord for that dream, because through that dream He gave me the theme for the next ministry coming up. I followed the leading of the Spirit and we saw great fruit in the ministry: many salvations, healings, deliverances. The kingdom was extended! It's wonderful to follow the leading of the Holy Spirit and be able to deliver "fresh bread" to God's people! This is just an example of the benefit released through a dream.

I WANT VISIONS!

> "...He reveals deep and mysterious things; He knows what is in the darkness, and the light dwells with Him." (Daniel 2:22).

Visions are another great way in which the Lord communicates with us. Like dreams, visions are also found plenty of times throughout the Scriptures.

When King Nebuchadnezzar had dreams that none of the magicians, the enchanters, the sorcerers of his kingdom could interpret, he started to make plans to destroy them. Fortunately, Daniel stepped up to the plate and told the king,

> "to appoint him a time, that he might show to the king the interpretation." (Daniel 2:16).

Daniel had the assurance that his God was able to communicate to him the interpretation of the king's dream. He told his companions,

> "to seek mercy of the God of heaven concerning this mystery, so that Daniel and his companions might not perish with the rest of the wise men of Babylon. Then the mystery was revealed to Daniel in a vision of the night." (Daniel 2:18-19).

Daniel asked the Lord for interpretation of the king's dream, and the Lord gave Daniel the interpretation of the dream through a vision. Proverbs 25:2 says,

> "It is the glory of God to conceal things, but the glory of kings is to search things out."

We have a "kingly anointing" since the day of our baptism to "search things out" in the Spirit!

Daniel told the king:

> "No wise men, enchanters, magicians , or astrologers can show to the king the mystery which the king has asked, but there is a God in heaven who reveals mysteries, and he has made known to King Nebuchadnezzar what will be in the latter days. Your dream and the visions of your head as you lay in bed are these...." (Daniel 2:27-28).

Brothers and sisters, we have the same God of Daniel. We need to flow in the same kind of assurance Daniel had! We need to "see" that the Lord is desiring to give us the revelation we need at a given time. We have the Holy Spirit living inside of us, Who releases to us the revelation that we need. He is "the spirit of wisdom and revelation" (Ephesians 1:17). The Holy Spirit

> "searches everything, even the depths of God" (1 Corinthians 2:10).

After Daniel correctly interpreted the king's dreams, the king said to Daniel,

> "...Truly, your God is God of gods and Lord of kings, and a revealer of mysteries, for you have been able to reveal this mystery. Then the king gave Daniel high honors and many great gifts, and made him ruler over the whole province of Babylon, and chief prefect over all the wise men of Babylon." (Daniel 2:47-48).

These are some New Testament examples of how the Lord used visions to communicate His heart:

> Through a vision the Holy Spirit directed Ananias to go pray with Saul (Acts 9:10).

If you read this passage you will see that Ananias interacted with the Lord. There was a flow of communication between them.

> Through a vision the Holy Spirit communicated with Peter to go to the house of Cornelius (Acts 10:10).

In verse 19 it says "And while Peter was pondering the vision, the Spirit said to him...." Peter pondered the vision; he pressed into it and the Lord spoke. In Acts 11:6, as he was recounting what happened, he said, speaking of the vision, "Looking at it closely I observed...." I am just trying to make the point that Peter 's eyes were focused on what the Lord was trying to show him.

> Through a vision the Holy Spirit instructed Paul to go to Macedonia (Acts 16:9-10).

The Lord used a vision for the preaching of the gospel in Macedonia.

Through a vision the Lord encouraged Paul to keep ministering in Corinth (Acts 18:9-10).

In the midst of great opposition, it was in a vision that the Lord gave Paul great words of comfort and encouragement.

We are living in times in which there has been a great acceleration in the Spirit; I believe that as we pray and wait on the Lord, and release our eyes to Him, there will be a greater flow of revelation, including visions.

I was praying for the son of a friend who needed a job. The Lord gave me a vision in which I saw angels coming down "Jacob's ladder" carrying something "heavy" in their hands. The Lord showed me that there was a job coming for my friend's son; not just a job, but an important one that carried "weight"! As my friend's son interviewed and waited, this vision helped him and his mother to believe and remain in peace, knowing that the Lord would fulfill what He had shown me. As I write this book, the vision has been fulfilled "far more abundantly" (Ephesians 3:20) than expected! Thank You, Jesus!

TURN AND SEE!

> "I will turn aside and see this great sight, why the bush is not burnt." (Exodus 3:3).

It was one more boring, unexciting day for Moses in the wilderness, keeping his father-in-law's flock, when he saw a flame of fire out of the midst of a bush. What was unusual was that "the bush was burning yet it was not consumed." (Exodus 3:2). It was not unusual to see a burning bush in the desert; what was unusual was that the bush was not being consumed. It caught Moses' attention. What did Moses do? He said

> "I will turn aside and see this great sight, why the bush is not burnt."

Moses did not ignore this unusual sight; he decided to check it out. In the same way, we must be sensitive to what "catches our attention." The moment that Moses decided to stop and look at the burning bush, something was set in motion in the Spirit realm:

> "When the Lord saw that he turned aside to see, God called to him out of the bush, Moses, Moses! And He said, Here am I."

It was when the Lord saw that Moses had turned aside to see, that He called Moses. It was there that the Lord identified Himself and commissioned Moses to deliver His people out of Egypt. The Lord does unexpected things when we least expect it at unexpected places! How sensitive are you to what's going on around you? Could it be possible that the Lord is waiting for you to "turn aside and see?" What is catching your attention?

In Acts 7:31, the point is also made that Moses "wandered at the sight; and as he drew near to look, the voice of the Lord came...." Again, the Holy Spirit makes the point that as Moses responded by drawing near to look, that the Lord spoke. I believe that in the "wilderness" the Lord wants to train our eyes to become sensitive to His leadings. We need to become so sensitive to the Holy Spirit that we learn to respond very quickly to His nudges.

In the first chapter of the book of Revelation, something similar happened to John; he heard a loud voice behind him and he decided to turn to see:

> "I was in the Spirit on the Lord's day, and I heard behind me a loud voice like a trumpet saying, 'Write what you see in a book and send it to the seven churches....' Then I turned to see the voice that was speaking to me, and on turning I saw seven golden lampstands, and in the midst of the lampstands one like a son of man, clothed with a long robe...." (Revelation 1:10-13).

It was on turning that John saw. The point that I'm trying to make is that we need to be sensitive to the Holy Spirit at all times so that we can "turn and see" what He wants to do. We must "turn aside" from our busyness to see what He might be trying to show us. Are you willing to stop what you're doing and instead "turn aside" to see what He wants to show you?

After the miraculous parting of the Red Sea, God's people were thirsty and could not drink the water of Marah because it was bitter. They grumbled (as usual) against Moses; but Moses cried to the Lord and the Lord

> "showed him a tree, and he threw it into the water, and the water became sweet." (Exodus 15:25).

Do you see the difference between the people and Moses? The people grumbled; Moses turned to the Lord! As Moses turned to the Lord, he positioned himself before the Lord to receive revelation and strategy of what he needed to do. In this case, the Holy Spirit showed Moses a tree; the Holy Spirit's "anointing" came on a tree, and by revelation Moses knew what to do. You don't have to keep drinking "bitter" waters; turn to the Lord, position yourself to receive revelation and strategy so that your water becomes "sweet." Grumbling and complaining are bitter ingredients in our diet! Praise and worship our beautiful Jesus and the valley of weeping will be changed into a "place of springs!" Instead of going from bad to worse you will go "from strength to strength!" (Psalm 84:6-7).

We need to position ourselves before the Lord with an attitude of thanksgiving, praise and worship throughout the day, for a continuous flow of revelation knowledge, so that we can partner with Him. No matter what the situation is, there is God's hidden agenda in it! Last year on the way to Uganda via Amsterdam, we lost our connecting flight and had to stay overnight in Amsterdam. As my brother and I walked through the airport, tired and jet-lagging, looking for the correct bus exit in order to go to the hotel, I kept thinking, "O.K. Lord, now what? What are You up to?" I had a sense that the Lord was the One who delayed our flight for some specific reason. Suddenly, I saw a strong, young, black airport employee and I felt led by the Spirit to ask him for help. I asked him to show us which exit to take. His accent was unmistakable; it was just like mine! I knew he was Cuban! I asked him where he came from, and of course, he said "Cuba." I knew this was a divine appointment! I started speaking to him in Spanish right away and said to him "What are the chances of three Cubans meeting in Amsterdam?" I shared with him how our plane had departed late from America and now we had lost our connection to Uganda. I told him that the Lord Himself had delayed our plane and set up this meeting so that he could meet Jesus! My Cuban friend was so touched! He repented and opened his heart for Jesus to come into his life as Lord and Savior! Brothers and sisters, doesn't the Good Shepherd leave ninety nine and goes for the lost one? Isn't this the heart of Christ? Everywhere we go there are lost sheep! Everywhere we go there are wounded, broken, hopeless, depressed individuals that are just waiting to have an encounter with the Lord, and you are the one that can lead them to Jesus! Yes, You! Open your eyes!

In Wellington, New Zealand, I was so surprised to see a street named "Cuba Street!" As soon as I saw that street, I sensed that the Holy Spirit had a "Cuba" plan up his sleeve. On my request, my friends took me on a Sunday to walk that street, but I did not sense the Holy Spirit showing me anything in particular. However, as we were leaving, I saw a nearby café called "Mi Cubita" with the Cuban flag painted on the wall. I knew that was the place and I knew that there was a Cuban in that island that needed to meet Jesus! On a Wednesday afternoon I ventured to walk the streets of Wellington with a missionary friend and one of my students. I had to find this Cuban man at all costs before I left Wellington! I knew there was a divine appointment with him prepared by the Holy Spirit! We visited several cafes with Cuban themes before going to "Mi Cubita." Once inside, I identified myself to the owner of this café, telling him that I was born in Cuba; I chatted with him and told him that I was there in Wellington to proclaim the Word of God. He was very gracious to us, treating us to coffee and cakes; the favor of God was upon us! Finally he came up to me with his cell phone and said "I know all the Cubans in this island; there are five of them and one is coming to the café right now." The three of us were ecstatic! We knew this was the man! When he showed up, it was just a matter of allowing the Holy Spirit to take the lead. We introduced ourselves, chatted and sipped coffee. It was a done deal; he repented, accepted Jesus in his heart as Lord and Savior and we prophesied over his life! I love Holy Spirit adventures, don't you?

In Acts 3, it was just one more afternoon as Peter and John "were going up to the temple at the hour of prayer." This was their usual routine; but this time, the Holy Spirit was up to something new! There was a lame man from birth that was placed daily at the gate of the temple; this was his day! The lame man asked Peter and John for alms and Peter "directed his gaze at him...." I believe that as Peter fixed his gaze on this man, the Holy Spirit revealed to Peter what the Lord wanted. What happened? A miraculous healing that brought 5,000 converts to Jesus! (Acts 4:4). Lamentations 3:22-23 says,

> "The steadfast love of the Lord never ceases, his mercies
> never come to an end;
> They are new every morning; great is thy faithfulness."

God's love, mercies, faithfulness are NEW every morning! He never runs out! There's a fresh supply of healings, deliverances, miracles at hand!

I was at the airport waiting for my flight, trying to find an empty seat in the gate area. As I searched for a seat, the Holy Spirit pointed out to me a young lady chatting away on her cell phone. Finally I told the Lord that I was willing to reach out to her and share with her the love of Jesus and the message of the gospel; however, there were no empty seats around her and she was talking non-stop. Suddenly, the airline agent announced that we had to move to another gate; quickly I picked up my stuff and headed for the newly assigned gate. I found an empty seat and sat; soon afterwards the young lady that the Lord had pointed out to me came and sat next to me. I knew this was a divine appointment! As I prayed silently in the Spirit, she was the one to open the conversation. Before I knew it I was sharing the love of Jesus and the message of salvation. She took a Bible out of her bag and said "I've been searching for the truth; I'm even carrying a Bible!"

She was ripe and open to the message of the gospel; I simply was God's assignment to bring her into the Kingdom. She repented and invited Jesus into her life as Lord and Savior. Alleluia! This young lady was at a crossroads in her life; a married man with children was after her and we prayed that she would be loosed from this relationship and for the right partner to come into her life. Do you think this was just a "coincidence?" Of course not! The Holy Spirit Himself changed the gates and planned the seating arrangement. Dear reader, everywhere you go, put on your "spiritual antennas" and allow the Holy Spirit to show you what He desires. Cultivate a sensitivity to the Holy Spirit and investigate what He is trying to show you.

As I was getting into a taxi with my friend to go to downtown Dar Es Salaam (Tanzania) for a radio/television program, immediately I sensed that the Lord wanted "business" with the taxi driver. I focused on the Lord and He showed me the pain in this young man's heart: it was the pain of living without Jesus! I "saw" that this young man was fed up with his life, fed up of driving taxis day in and day out. I saw how empty and meaningless his life was. I started to minister to him the love of Jesus and told him that only Jesus could satisfy his heart. I started to explain that the salvation that Jesus offers starts in this planet the moment we repent and turn to Him. The Lord gave me a vision of this young man, dressed very nicely, working in a managerial position in a company. I gave witness to what the Lord was showing me and what Jesus had done in my life. When we arrived at our destination, he was ready for prayer. He repented, gave his life to Jesus, and we laid hands on him and prayed for the Holy Spirit to come in power. After the radio/television interview was completed, I was surprised to see that this young man had been waiting for us to take us back home. On the way home, the Lord instructed me to invite this young man to the upcoming seminar in Agape Centre, which was starting precisely that same night. I told him that if he wanted to go to the week-long seminar, I myself would pay for it. He replied, "I am ready for it!" This young man came to the seminar and his life was changed! You could see the glory of the Lord all over his face! He gave testimony and said that he was a drunkard but had made a decision to leave that lifestyle behind and follow Jesus! His own father decided to come over and see for himself if this was true; he could not recognize his own son because his face was totally changed. This young man asked me if he could stay for the next week-long seminar and I gladly paid for it! Glory to God! Everywhere that we go there is a harvest to be brought in! Turn to the Lord and let Him show you what He wants!

LORD, SHOW ME YOUR GLORY!

> "Holy, holy, holy, is the Lord of hosts; the whole earth is full of his glory." (Isaiah 6:3).

Isaiah was a holy man; a priest and a prophet. What changed him? An encounter with the Lord, where he saw the Lord sitting on His throne:

> "In the year that King Uzziah died, I saw the Lord sitting upon a throne, high and lifted up; and his train filled the temple. Above him stood the seraphim...and the foundations of the thresholds shook at the voice of him who called and the house was filled with smoke."
> (Isaiah 6:1-4).

What happened to Isaiah after he "saw" the Lord in His glory? Amazing things happened! First of all, Isaiah recognized his need for cleansing. He said,

> "Woe is me! For I am lost; for I am a man of unclean lips...."

Second of all, the Lord Himself provided for Isaiah's cleansing:

> "Then flew one of the seraphim to me, having in his hand a burning coal which he had taken with tongs from the altar. And he touched my mouth, and said: "Behold, this has touched your lips; your guilt is taken away, and your sin forgiven."

Thirdly, Isaiah freely volunteered his service to the Lord:

> "And I heard the voice of the Lord saying, "Whom shall I send, and who will go for us?" Then I said, "Here am I! Send me."

Isaiah's call and response started with "seeing!" We were meant to see, to experience, to have personal revelation of the Lord, to experience and carry the glory.

Peter had a similar response to the Lord, but in a totally different setting! It was not in a "holy" place like with Isaiah, but in an ordinary setting; by a lake surrounded with people. In Luke 5, when Peter saw the miraculous catch of fish,

> "...he fell down at Jesus' knees, saying, Depart from me, for I am a sinful man, O Lord."

Like Isaiah, when Peter encountered the Lord, he realized his sinfulness. However, the Lord invited him to "catch" men and Peter left everything and followed Jesus. Like Isaiah, it took a "seeing" for Peter to leave everything to follow the Lord.

We cannot limit the Lord! He will manifest Himself to whoever and wherever He pleases! No matter the setting, the Lord manifests His glory in whatever way He wants! Think that the King of Glory was born in a smelly cave!

Solomon was commissioned to build a temple for the Lord and he fulfilled that mandate. After he finished building the temple, he brought in the ark of the Lord and offered great sacrifices to the Lord, with lots of praise and worship. The cloud of glory appeared and left everyone undone:

> "...and when the song was raised, with trumpets and cymbals and other musical instruments, in praise to the Lord, for he is good, for his steadfast love endures forever, the house, the house of the Lord, was filled with a cloud, so that the priests could not stand to minister because of the cloud; for the glory of the Lord filled the house of God." (2 Chronicles 5:13).

Something happened when the priests saw and experienced the cloud of glory; they could not stand to minister because of the mighty presence of the Lord! The Lord made His presence seen and felt! It was undeniable that He was present. There is something about completing a God-given task; He Himself affirms it and He shows up! It was the same with Moses when he finished building the tabernacle in the desert:

> "...So Moses finished the work. Then the cloud covered the tent of meeting and the glory of the Lord filled the tabernacle. And Moses was not able to enter the tent of meeting, because the cloud abode upon it, and the glory of the Lord filled the tabernacle." (Exodus 40:34-35).

It was the longing of Moses to see God's glory:

> Moses said, "I pray thee, show me thy glory."
> (Exodus 33:18).

We too have a mandate from the Lord, and it is to proclaim His glorious gospel to all creation (Mark 16:15). When we step out in faith to do what He has told us to do, He confirms it with His glorious presence! We are living in days that the Lord is manifesting His glory! What is God's glory? Who He is! Everything that He is! The fullness of Who He is! There are many manifestations of His glorious presence: His majesty and splendor; His goodness; great joy, healings, love, conviction of sin, freedom, revelation, deliverances, visions, provision, angelic presence, miracles. In the glory we experience His abundant life; His glory breaks the power of sin and sickness. In the realm of the glory, miracles happen without the laying on of hands! It's the atmosphere of breakthroughs for any area in our lives! In the 2008 WOW conference in Emmaus Centre in Uganda, we experienced the glory realm: a lady's tumor dissolved just by being in the glory; one lady's eyesight totally restored (without the laying on of hands!); a marriage restored; great joy and laughter; healed minds and emotions; freedom from multiple pains. I personally have a longing and a hunger, a desire to be in His glory presence and experience Him again and again! Like Moses, I want Him to show me more and more of His glory! It's in His presence that we are transformed into His image, from one degree of glory to another! (2 Corinthians 3:18).

Again this summer in Agape Centre, Tanzania, we experienced the realm of God's glory; it was like a Holy Spirit invasion of His presence. Heaven invaded earth, the schedule was disrupted and most everyone landed on the floor, just like the priests in Solomon's temple who could not stand because of the weight of His glory! What was the fruit? A greater desire and hunger for the Lord! A sense of awe and amazement that left everyone speechless!

Why is it important to manifest God's glory? Because of the increasing darkness in the world; as we manifest His glory, the Lord will attract the lost to us. That's why Isaiah says,

> "Arise, shine; for your light has come, and the glory of the Lord has risen upon you.
> For behold, darkness shall cover the earth, and thick darkness the peoples;
> But the Lord will arise upon you, and his glory will be seen upon you.
> And nations shall come to your light, and kings to the brightness of your rising.
> Lift up your eyes round about, and see, they all gather together, they come to you…" (Isaiah 60:1-4).

The world is already in "thick darkness;" but the light of God's glory shines brighter and brighter in ever increasing darkness! As we arise, we will shine and the glory of the Lord will be seen upon us; "nations" will come to our light. As the darkness increases, we will shine for the sake of Jesus! This is the time of the great harvest! We must lift up our eyes from the circumstances surrounding us and "see how the fields are already white for harvest." (John 4:35).

I was at the airport waiting to board my plane. The gate was packed with people. There was a group of three sitting near me; it was obvious that the older lady of that group had something wrong with her eyes. I could tell she was in great pain; she could not sit still and kept placing something like a napkin over her eyes. I started to pray in the Spirit, waiting for the Holy Spirit's direction. As her sister walked by me, I took the initiative and said to her, " I know there is something wrong with your friend; I am a Catholic charismatic and I pray for the sick in the name of Jesus. If your friend wants, I will pray for her." Within minutes, there I was, sitting next to this lady, laying my hands on her and releasing the healing of the kingdom into her eyes. I took authority over the pain and commanded it to leave her eyes in Jesus' name. All "eyes" in that gate area were on us! People around us were staring and watching as I laid hands on her! After a few minutes the pain started to leave her eyes and when done, I left her sitting still and in peace like a baby! The pain left! My friends, Jesus never fails! He's just looking for His people to move in faith. I moved in confidence because I know that my God is a good God, a healer and restorer, and has commissioned us to "heal the sick." (Matthew 10:7-8). This is just an example of how we can release His glory! This lady was a lukewarm Catholic; as I prayed with her I explained how Jesus the healer is the same yesterday, today and forever and the fact that He uses little people on earth to carry on with His works. I explained also how she needed to open her heart to Jesus in a new way and cultivate a relationship with Him.

It's God's desire to fill the earth with His glory! His people on earth, you and I, are to release His glory everywhere we go so that people can "see" the reality of our God. It's the atmosphere of heaven invading earth!

> "...all the earth shall be filled with the glory of the Lord." (Numbers 14:20).

We are the ones the Holy Spirit uses to fill the earth with His glory! We are His temples, we carry the glory within us! King Jesus lives within us and we release His presence wherever we go! We need this revelation to step up to the plate and be who we were created to be!

"For the earth will be filled with the knowledge of the glory of the Lord, as the waters cover the sea." (Habakkuk 2:14).

LORD, SHOW ME THE INVISIBLE REALM!

"Then Elisha prayed, and said, 'O Lord, I pray thee, open his eyes that he may see.'" (2 Kings 6:17).

Elisha's servant was gripped with fear when he saw with his natural eyes the enemy army surrounding them with horses and chariots. The prophet told him,

"Fear not, for those who are with us are more than those who are with them."

Elisha then asked the Lord to open his servant's eyes so that he could see the reality of the spiritual world and not fear. This is what happened:

"So the Lord opened the eyes of the young man, and he saw; and behold, the mountain was full of horses and chariots of fire round about Elisha."

The servant's eyes needed to be opened so that he could see the spiritual realm, which is the one that lasts; when he saw it, he was no longer gripped by fear! What a comfort that we have angels on assignment protecting us as we serve the Lord.

St. Paul says,

"...we look not to the things that are seen but to the things that are unseen; for the things that are seen are transient, but the things that are unseen are eternal." (2 Corinthians 4:18).

Brothers and sisters, our reality is the kingdom of God! It's not what we see with our natural eyes! The Lord encourages us to ask Him to show us things that we cannot see with our natural eyes:

"Call to me and I will answer you, and will tell you great and hidden things which you have not known." (Jeremiah 33:3).

Revelation knowledge is not just about angels, of course, but also revelation of just about anything that has to do with the kingdom! We need more revelation of heaven, praise and worship, angels, healing, the heart of the Father, the joy of the Lord, etc. The Holy Spirit has given us revelatory gifts so that we can minister effectively to God's people; words of knowledge, words of wisdom, discernment of spirits, gift of prophecy, dreams and visions. We can certainly ask the Lord to show us what He wants to do in a meeting. The Lord desires that we ask Him what His plans are, so that we can co-labor effectively with Him. We can ask Him for revelation when praying with individuals, groups, cities, nations. In a recent ministry in Seattle, the Lord "showed" me through a word of knowledge before the meeting that He wanted to save some marriages. In the meeting I called to the front all the married couples, and was amazed at the amount of couples that came forward! We blessed the couples and then I started to minister to the marriages in trouble; many started to weep (including men!) and were visibly touched by the Holy Spirit. At the end of the meeting, three couples that were not married sacramentally decided they would put their lives in order and made a decision that night to marry in Church! When the Holy Spirit ministers, people receive revelation and conviction to do the right thing! There is much fruit!

Last summer in the 2009 WOW conference in Uganda, the Lord spoke to me before the conference and showed me that this WOW would be filled with "Esthers!" Indeed, I had to have my eyes opened to receive that revelation in order to minister effectively to His people. With my natural eyes I didn't see any Esthers; but with the eyes of my heart the Lord showed me what was "hidden." It turned out that present in that group of women were two members of Parliament from Sudan; the secretary of health; an overseer for the school system; a politician; and other women in places of authority in the government. In addition, many prayer group leaders and young people whom the Lord is grooming to extend His kingdom in Africa attended this conference. They all left revived, renewed, restored, fired-up, empowered, but most of all, they knew for certain that they were alive "for such a time as this." (Esther 4:14).

Hagar, Abraham's slave and the mother of his son Ishmael, had to have her eyes opened so that she could see that the Lord had provided her with water. Together with her son Ishmael, she was sent away with bread and a skin of water into the wilderness (Genesis 21:14-21). The water ran out and she became despondent thinking that Ishmael would die of thirst. Ishmael wept and "God heard the voice of the lad...." The angel of the Lord ministered to Hagar. Look at what the Lord did:

> "Then God opened her eyes, and she saw a well of water; and she went, and filled the skin with water, and gave the lad a drink." (V.19).

Let's ask the Lord to open our eyes to His provision and strategy every time we encounter a setback or a problem. Every difficulty is an excuse for a miracle! We walk by faith and not by sight, so our eyes have to be kept on the Lord and not on the difficulty; on the promise and not the problem! At times desperation can be a good thing: it will propel us to the solution and breakthrough as we look to the Lord for it.

> "To thee I lift up my eyes, O thou who art enthroned in the heavens! Behold, as the eyes of servants look to the hand of their master, as the eyes of a maid to the hand of her mistress, so our eyes look to the Lord our God, till he have mercy upon us." (Psalm 123:1-2).

LORD, SHOW ME MY INHERITANCE!

> "The Lord said to Abram...'Lift up your eyes, and look from the place where you are, northward and southward and eastward and westward; for all the land which you see I will give to you and to your descendants forever.'" (Genesis 13:14-15).

It's important that we see with our spiritual eyes the plans and purposes the Lord has for our lives. Every single believer has a ministry! The Lord basically told Abraham that what he saw was his! How big is your vision? We're living in times in which the Holy Spirit is expanding our vision, because we have been thinking too small! There is an "inheritance" for every believer. If we think big, we'll receive big; if we shrink God we'll receive a shrunken version of His plan. The devil is a "destiny robber" who lies and tries to block our way into God's plans and purposes for our lives. As God's people, we need to "see" ourselves as people of the Kingdom; He has "made us a kingdom" (Revelation 1:6; 5:10) and we are the ones that carry out His plans and purposes on earth. Peter says,

> "But you are a chosen race, a royal priesthood, a holy nation, God's own people, that you may declare the wonderful deeds of him who called you out of darkness into his marvelous light. Once you were no people but now you are God's people…." (1 Peter 2:9-10).

We are His ambassadors (2 Corinthians 5:20) and we are to represent and extend His Kingdom on earth and enforce the victory of Calvary. Will there be opposition? Of course! This is why we must "see" with our spiritual eyes the vision God has for our lives and believe it. He expects us to renew our minds so that we can think like He thinks. The Word of God expands our minds so that we can see that in the Lord there are unlimited possibilities.

> "For with God nothing will be impossible." (Luke 1:37).

Jesus said in Mark 9:23b,

> "All things are possible to him who believes."

The Virgin Mary believed first and then she conceived Jesus in her womb. It took great faith for Mary to believe that by the power of the Holy Spirit she would conceive supernaturally the Savior of the world! That's why Elizabeth said "And blessed is she who believed …." (Luke 1:45).

Moses was able to leave behind the riches of Egypt because he saw with his spiritual eyes something greater that God had for him:

> "By faith Moses, when he was grown up, refused to be called the son of Pharaoh's daughter, choosing rather to share ill-treatment with the people of God than to enjoy the fleeting pleasures of sin. He considered abuse suffered for the Christ greater wealth than the treasures of Egypt, for he looked to the reward. By faith he left Egypt, not being afraid of the anger of the king; for he endured as seeing him who is invisible." (Hebrews 11:24-27).

How could Moses leave behind the kind of life he had in Egypt and choose instead "ill-treatment" and "abuse" with the people of God? He had revelation! Revelation of the one true God! He "saw" the true treasure, Jesus Christ, and everything that the world had to offer could not compare to Him!

At a time in my life when I was surrounded by "mountains of impossibilities," I woke up from sleep one night and looked at the clock; it was 1:45 a.m. I turned to the Lord to receive revelation and He showed me it was Luke 1:45!

> "And blessed is she who believed that there would be a fulfillment of what was spoken to her from the Lord."

Yes, the Lord was calling me to believe, to believe that He was the God of the impossible! I was facing a court battle that humanly speaking, it was impossible to win. At that moment in my life I had no home, no money. My heart was broken because my four children could not stay together with me. The Lord Himself encouraged me to believe, so that I could "see" victory ahead! Victory is what I eventually received in court! That victory has enabled me to serve the Lord full time and go wherever He sends me. You see, our job is to believe; we must capture the revelation of His plan with the "eyes of our hearts" (Ephesians 1:18) and believe what He shows us, no matter how impossible it is to our human mind. Brothers and sisters, there will always be a battle at the gate of our prophetic destiny; the enemy doesn't want us to enter in! Our job is to capture the revelation of what the Lord wants for our lives and go for it! Believe, nurture your faith and be a doer of His Word, and you will enter into God's plan and inheritance for your life!

> "What no eye has seen, nor ear heard, nor the heart of man conceived, what God has prepared for those who love him." (1 Corinthians 2:9).

In 2007 while in Uganda, the Lord told me to reach out to the pygmies. In 2008 I went to the pygmies, in obedience to His voice. What I encountered touched my heart: a people group that is rejected, neglected, depressed, impoverished, sick, dirty and suffering from malnutrition. They have no skills to enter the mainstream of society. They are small, skinny and hopeless. Their "houses" are made of grass and mud. There is no water, no electricity. Our pets in America have a much nicer life that what these people have! I was shaken by this! As I was preaching the Gospel to them and telling them about the love of Jesus and the power of His Blood, I could see that they could not believe the "Good News" because they had never experienced goodness from anybody. I felt I was getting nowhere with the pygmies, until I heard the voice of the Lord telling me "Romans 8:32." I shared with them Romans 8:32:

> "He who did not spare His own Son but gave Him up for us all, will He not also give us all things with Him?"

The Lord was showing me that He would give them anything they desired! I looked into their eyes and said to them "What do you want? What do you hold dear in your hearts? What is the desire of your hearts?" No one said a word; they just stared at me in hopelessness. I told them that the biggest gift is Jesus; the Son of God that died for our salvation. I told them that God the Father had already provided for our biggest need: a Savior. All other things that we need is nothing in comparison to Jesus. They kept looking at me until the oldest pygmy spoke up and said "I would like a house; ours are falling apart; I would also like a cow so that I could drink milk every day."

My friend Fr. Fokushaba and the interpreter figured out how much a wooden house would cost; totally affordable with American dollars! I realized then that the Lord had taken me there so that these pygmies could have decent little houses and cows! Amazing! The day ended in victory: all of them turned to Jesus. There was an outbreak of joy and dancing and they were filled with hope! I told them that they needed to pray for me so that people in America would respond to their desire for new houses. I committed myself with the Lord to build them ten houses; I already have money for fifteen houses and eight houses are already built! The money has come into my hands effortlessly, because it is a GOD-THING!

Brothers and sisters, the Lord has amazing things prepared for the people that love Him! This new life starts down here, in this planet. It's God's desire to reveal to us the amazing plans He has for us. We are kingdom people anointed to carry on with the works of Jesus. As a matter of fact, if we don't have a prophetic vision of His plans and purposes for our lives, we are going to go around in circles, like the Israelites in the desert, never entering into our destiny down here:

> "Where there is no vision, the people get out of hand...." (Proverbs 29:18) (NJB).

Without a vision for our lives, we will be fruitless! We will not be able to move forward! Without a vision, we lose heart, direction, purpose. The Apostle Paul exhorted his friend Archippus in this way:

> "And say to Archippus, 'See that you fulfill the ministry which you have received in the Lord.'" (Colossians 4:17).

Just before the prophet Elijah was taken into heaven, Elijah told his disciple Elisha:

> "Ask what I shall do for you, before I am taken from you.

And Elisha said,
I pray you, let me inherit a double share of your spirit.
And he said,
You have asked a hard thing; yet, if you see me as I am being taken from you,
It shall be so for you; but if you do not see me, it shall not be so." (2 Kings 2:9-10).

What was Elijah's condition for Elisha to receive a double portion of his spirit?

That Elisha would SEE him as he was taken up! Elijah was Elisha's spiritual father, and as a first born son (in the Spirit), Elisha was entitled to a double portion of the inheritance; in this case, a double portion of Elijah's ministry (see Deut. 21:17). When the chariot of fire and horses of fire came down and separated them, Elijah was taken up in a whirlwind and Elisha saw it and cried,

"My father, my father! The chariots of Israel and its horsemen!"

Elisha "saw" and moved accordingly; he immediately "took the mantle of Elijah…." (2 Kings 2:13).

III

FOCUS: PROBLEM OR PROMISE?

> "If then you, have been raised with Christ, seek the things that are above, where Christ is, seated at the right hand of God. Set your mind on things that are above, not on things that are on earth." (Colossians 3:1-2).

The Apostle Paul tells us that we're supposed to be seeking the things above and setting our minds on them, not on the things of this earth. This is a constant thing that we must do. The enemy would have us do the opposite: to concentrate on earthly things, problems and difficulties and employ our minds to formulate human solutions, rather than turning to the Lord for answers, strategies and revelation. We need to start using our imagination in godly ways for the sake of the kingdom. We must learn to engage our imagination on things above. Imagine thousands turning to Jesus; imagine amazing healings and miracles; imagine the unity of the Body of Christ; imagine yourself loving the unlovely; imagine the joy of heaven; imagine the four living creatures, the twenty-four elders!

One of the enemy's most successful tactics to keep us defeated and discouraged is to get us to think and ponder on the problem all day long, rather than to focus on the promise. Fixing our eyes on the problem will result in more darkness released into our lives. The more we think about how terrible and difficult the situation is, the more hopeless and depressed we become.

Instead, we are to focus on God's promise, which is the solution. We are to ask the Lord for strategy and for revelation of what we need to act upon so we can see His plan unfold in our lives and through us. We need to "see" from His perspective. According to the above verse, we should be seeking and setting our minds on things that are above! Get your Bible and get your mind renewed (Romans 12:2)! Again in Phillipians 4: 8 the Apostle Paul makes this very clear:

> "Finally, brethren, whatever is true, whatever is honorable, whatever is just, whatever is pure, whatever is lovely, whatever is gracious, if there is any excellence, if there is anything worthy of praise, think about these things."

I know only one person who fits these categories: JESUS! Like the Virgin Mary, we are to ponder in our hearts, contemplate and meditate on everything that has to do with Jesus (Luke 2:19, 51).

Moses knew the importance of controlling the eye gate; look at what the Lord told him:

> "The Lord said to Moses, 'Speak to the people of Israel, and bid them to make tassels on the corners of the garments throughout their generations, and to put upon the tassel of each corner a cord of blue; and it shall be to you a tassel to look upon and remember all the commandments of the Lord, to do them, not to follow after your own heart and your own eyes, which you are inclined to go after wantonly. So you shall remember and do all my commandments, and be holy to your God.'"
> (Numbers 15:37-40).

According to the Lord, the way we use our eyes will determine which direction we take: holiness or perdition!

The story of King Jehoshaphat in 2 Chronicles 20 is a powerful one. He was being attacked by three armies more powerful than his. The Bible says in v. 3 that he "feared, and set himself to seek the Lord...." WE see that the King did not allow "fear" to control him; he decided to seek the Lord instead. In verse 12 the King tells the Lord,

> "...For we are powerless against this great multitude that is coming against us. We do not know what to do, but our eyes are upon thee."

Psalm 25:15 says,

> "My eyes are ever toward the Lord, for He will pluck my feet out of the net."

Numbers 21 gives us a very good visual of what we are to do when "bitten" by the enemy: STOP looking at the problem and lift up your eyes to look to JESUS!

In Numbers 21:4-9, God's people became impatient and started to grumble and complain "against God and Moses." They lost their vision of the Promised Land, which was their God-given destiny; they complained about God's provision and even grumbled about the manna, calling it "worthless food." Fiery serpents were released against them; many people died because of the snake bites. They repented for their negative words and turned to Moses for help. This is what the Lord told Moses to do:

> "Make a fiery serpent, and set it on a pole; and every one who is bitten, when he sees it, shall live."
> (Numbers 21:8).

What was God's solution? To set up a fiery serpent on a pole and have the victims look up (with their eyes) and see it. Of course, this points to Jesus hanging on the Cross, becoming sin for us (2 Corinthians 5:21), so that every one

> "who sees the Son and believes in him should have eternal life...." (John 6:40).

Moses obeyed the Lord; he set up the pole with the serpent,

"and if a serpent bit any man, he would look at the bronze serpent and live." (Numbers 21:9).

Do you see the God-dynamics taking place in this passage of Scripture? Those who that had grumbled and complained and now were bitten by the serpents, had to take their eyes off the serpents that were released against them, and instead they had to lift up their eyes to look at God's provision: in this case the serpent on the pole. They had to trust the Lord as they lifted up their eyes to the solution, because now they couldn't defend themselves against the snakes that were writhing on the floor next to them! In the same way, when we're going through a tough time, quit looking at the problem and lift up your eyes to the Lord! Don't try to fix it yourself. Look to Him and He will speak to you, give you revelation and strategy for your particular situation. I am not saying to live in denial! No, we must know what is going on but we must also know that in Christ we have everything we need! We are not orphans! Colossians 2:3 says that in Christ,

"are hid all the treasures of wisdom and knowledge."

Do you think that He has what you need for your particular situation? We must lift up our eyes to the Lord and start thanking and praising Him! Doesn't make sense to the carnal mind, but this is what we must do! It's the atmosphere of praise and worship that the Lord inhabits (Psalm 22:3) and where there is a release of revelation for your situation. Get into God's Word and allow the Holy Spirit to renew your mind, so that you can think like God thinks! Look at Psalm 121:

"I lift up my eyes to the hills, from whence does my help come?
My help comes from the Lord, who made heaven and earth.
He will not let your foot be moved, He who keeps you will not slumber.
Behold, he who keeps Israel will neither slumber nor sleep....

The Lord will keep you from all evil; he will keep your
life.
The Lord will keep your going out and your coming in
from this time forth and for evermore."

Again, it's at that moment of difficulty that our eyes need to be lifted up to the Lord and we not allow ourselves to become distracted, discouraged and distressed by the circumstances in our lives. As we enthrone Him in our praises and our eyes are fixed on Him, we realize that the maker of heaven and earth is bigger and more powerful than any trial or difficulty in our lives. In His presence our problems shrink because we regain the correct perspective! The correct perspective is that He has already triumphed at the Cross! We start seeing as He sees!

Renewing our mind with the Word of God and praising and worshiping the Lord will help us keep our eyes lifted up to the Lord. It will help us to not waver in faith, but like Abraham, we'll grow strong in faith giving glory to God, "fully convinced that God is able to do what he had promised." (Romans 5:20-21). It will help us flow in the rivers of the Spirit as we enter into His presence (Psalm 100:4). "Wells" of joy, revelation, restoration, etc. will break open in His presence and release what is needed at the moment. In an atmosphere of praise and worship, there is an acceleration of the Holy Spirit to confirm God's Word and extend God's kingdom on earth as it is in heaven. Look at what the prophet Amos (Amos 9: 13-14) says will happen when the Tabernacle of David (24 hours of praise and worship) is restored:

"possess the remnant of Edom..." (victory).

"the plowman shall overtake the reaper..." (acceleration).

"the mountains shall drip sweet wine..." (revelation).

"restore the fortunes..." (restoration).

"rebuild the ruined cities and inhabit them..." (restoration).

"plant vineyards and drink their wine..." (satisfaction).

"make gardens and eat their fruit..." (fruitfulness).

Last year in the Uganda 2009 WOW, in an atmosphere of great praise and worship, a distraught mother asked for prayer because she had just received a message that her teenage son was missing. He had not returned home for several days. The congregation prayed with expectant faith for the safe return of her son; we thanked and praised the Lord for His love and mercy. Within twenty-four hours that boy returned home safe and sound! In an atmosphere of high praise and worship, victory was released! Another lady asked for prayer for her strayed husband, who had left her for another woman a while ago. Before the conference was over, the husband showed up in the conference, and publicly repented for the sin of adultery! In an atmosphere of high praise and worship, a miracle of restoration was released! A word of knowledge was released that there would be reconciliation between rebellious daughters and their mothers; just in the lunch break, within an hour, four or five rebellious daughters rang their mothers to reconcile! Do you "see" the acceleration that praise and worship releases? Through a word of knowledge sick husbands at home received healing! These are just some of the testimonies that we witnessed as we worshiped the Lord in spirit and truth and kept our eyes lifted up to the Lord!

Truly when we praise and worship the Lord, we position ourselves in a place where He can come (Psalm 22:3) to rule and reign in our midst! It's heaven invading earth! As He moves in power our eyes are fixed on Him!

I love the story of Gideon. He had an encounter with the Lord that changed his life. The Lord found him in a place of fear and hiding and called him "mighty man of valor." (Judges 6:12) He was used mightily by God to deliver Israel from the Midianites with a reduced army of three hundred men. The Lord gave Gideon the strategy for victory and this is what Gideon told his men before they went to battle:

"Look at me, and do likewise…."

One thing was required of Gideon's men: they had to keep their eyes on Gideon and do exactly what he was doing. This was a good thing after all; the little army of three hundred was so outnumbered by the enemy, that if they focused on the enemy army most probably they would faint! But this is the key to victory: as we believe His Word and stand on it, the Lord fights for us! It's not about our own power or influence; it's not about our manmade strategies or plans! It's about the Lord Himself fighting for us and receiving the glory due His Name!

> "His delight is not in the strength of the horse; nor his pleasure in the legs of a man;
> But the Lord takes pleasure in those who fear him, in those who hope in his steadfast love."
> (Psalm 147:10-11).

> "Some boast of chariots, and some of horses; but we boast of the name of the Lord our God.
> They will collapse and fall; but we shall rise and stand upright." (Psalm 20: 7-8).

The story of Peter walking on water has the same message: keep your eyes on the Lord and not on the problem! Peter walked on water as long as he kept his eyes fixed on the Lord, but

> "when he saw the wind, he was afraid and beginning to sink he cried out…." (Matthew 14: 28-31).

I'll give you a word of wisdom: If you're going through a tough time, hang out only with people of faith!

Hang out with people that will help you stay focused on the Lord and encourage you to believe God for the impossible; people who hear from God and can speak life into you through a prophetic word.

Last year on the way to Arua from Kampala, my friend Tessa and I took a small plane to our destination. Before we boarded we prayed for traveling mercies and thanked God for a safe arrival. There was one stop before reaching Arua. We were headed to Yumbe, a town where two years ago we had seen amazing miracles and Muslims turning to Jesus. In the middle of the flight, our small plane was just going around in circles; it was cloudy and foggy and we could see nothing! The radar kept going off warning the pilot of the terrain around us; it was a hilly area. Immediately we took authority in Jesus' name over the negative weather patterns, commanded the clouds and fog to depart in Jesus' name, prayed in tongues and praised the Lord for the remainder of the journey. The plane was never able to make it to its first stop; but finally we arrived safely in Arua forty minutes late. The enemy tried to stop this outreach, but he couldn't. As we kept our eyes on Jesus and kept focused on the fact that greater is he that is in us than he who is in the world (1 John 4:4), we were able to stay calm and release our authority over the enemy. Of course, the enemy didn't want the kingdom of God extended in Yumbe, a town highly populated by Muslims!

IV

READY FOR BATTLE!

LORD, OPEN MY EYES TO WAR! NO MORE PASSIVITY!

"For we are not contending against flesh and blood, but against the principalities, against the powers, against the world rulers of this present darkness, against the spiritual hosts of wickedness in the heavenly places." (Ephesians 6:12).

We are in a war whether we like it or not, whether we know it or not! Ignorance of this truth can be a deadly! I say it's time to enforce the victory of Calvary! The prophet Hosea says,

"My people are destroyed for lack of knowledge...." (Hosea 4:6).

Isaiah says,

"Therefore my people go into exile for want of knowledge...." (Isaiah 5:13).

"But this is a people robbed and plundered, they are all of them trapped in holes and hidden in prisons; they have become a prey with none to rescue, a spoil with none to say, Restore!" (Isaiah 42:22).

This is why we need our eyes to be opened to this truth: we

are in a battle but we are not contending against human beings, but against the invisible, demonic forces behind the negative situations that we encounter. Because this is a spiritual battle, we need to fight with spiritual weapons! There are demonic forces over nations, regions, cities, families, individuals, etc. that war against the purposes of the King, His Kingdom, His people. The enemy comes to "steal and kill and destroy" (John 10:10); this is his job description. Many times God gets the blame for the works of the devil! This is because of ignorance of the Scriptures!

The good news is that Jesus has already defeated the enemy (Colossians 2:15), so what we must do is enforce the victory of Calvary in every situation that is not in alignment with the Word of God. For this purpose we have been anointed, empowered, gifted. Jesus made it very clear to His followers that they should not leave Jerusalem, but "wait for the promise of the Father...." What was, and is, the "promise of the Father?" THE HOLY SPIRIT! On Pentecost they would receive the Holy Spirit and power. Jesus told them (Acts 1:8),

> "But you shall receive power when the Holy Spirit has come upon you; and you shall be my witnesses in Jerusalem and in all Judea and Samaria and to the end of the earth."

To be a "witness" of Jesus Christ is not the same as being a passive, pew-warming spectator! To be a witness means that you are even willing to die for Jesus and be a martyr! To be a witness means that you are light in the midst of darkness, truth in the midst of lies, salt in the midst of decay! To be a witness means to be bold and fearless in the face of opposition! Church, wake up!

Jesus said in Luke 10:19,

> "Behold, I have given you authority to tread upon serpents and scorpions, and over all the power of the enemy; and nothing shall hurt you."

We have HIS authority! We are to release it where it is needed. We "war" from a position of rest and victory, because the Lord

> "has raised us up with him, and made us sit with him in the heavenly places in Christ Jesus...." (Ephesians 2:6).

If you notice, Jesus is seated in heavenly places; in the Spirit realm we are seated with Him, "far above all rule and authority and power and dominion, and above every name that is named...." (Ephesians 1:20-21). The enemy is under our feet! We are not under any circumstance, but over all of them! We are not a band of helpless, powerless orphans! On the contrary, we are ambassadors for Christ (2 Corinthians 5:20) and more than conquerors in Christ! (Romans 8:37). We have been clothed with power from on high! (Luke 2:49).

It is through the Church, us, that the Kingdom of God advances and extends; it is through us that the Lord rules and reigns in this planet. Look at what the Apostle Paul says in Ephesians 3:8-10:

> "To me, though I am the very least of all the saints, this grace was given, to preach to the Gentiles the unsearchable riches of Christ, and to make all men see what is the plan of the mystery hidden for ages in God who created all things; that through the church the manifold wisdom of God might now be made known to the principalities and powers in the heavenly places."

What is the "mystery" that Paul is trying to make all men see? The fact that it is "through the church" that God makes known His wisdom to the "principalities and powers in the heavenly places." Who is the church: believers! You and me!

This is why we cannot remain as passive spectators any longer! If we don't advance the Kingdom of God, the enemy will keep advancing his! Brothers and sisters, there is no vacuum in the spirit realm; either we take over, or the enemy takes over! Like David, it's time to face and fight the "giants" in our lives, families, churches, cities and nation!

Look at the signs of the times; let's not be blind as to how the enemy has advanced in our nation: increase of abortions, sexual immorality of every type, pornography, child-sex trafficking, violence, murder, suicides, addictions. Last week in the high school that I graduated from a student was stabbed to death by another student during school hours! People are gripped with fear, anxiety and panic attacks; depression, discouragement and hopelessness abounds. There has been an increase of bad fruit because of godlessness, resulting in a great moral decay of our society and culture. Jesus rebuked the people for not knowing how to interpret the times:

> "You hypocrites! You know how to interpret the appearance of earth and sky; but why do you not know how to interpret the present time?" (Luke 12:56).

9/11 was an eye opener for many, but I'm afraid most people are still asleep to the fact that radical Islam is not only a big threat to America but to the entire world; they want to take over! The spirit of Islam is not the Holy Spirit! The Muslims have been infiltrating the nations around the world, strategizing, and using their money quite effectively to win people to their faith. In Africa, for example, poverty is fertile ground for them to come and "seduce" people into their camp with jobs, houses, bonuses, etc. As I travel in Africa, I'm seeing an increasing Muslim presence; Muslims and mosques are everywhere! Many Christians are falling into this trap because of the promise of a better life. In the Western world their strategies might be different, but their goal is the same: to take over! As the people of God we need to start praying that this "Muslim advance" be stopped; we need to love them into God's kingdom; we need to proclaim and demonstrate the power of the Gospel with signs and wonders followings so that they turn to Jesus! Church, it's time to step up to the plate!

I say it's time to interpret the present time! It's time for WAR! It's time to take back what the enemy has stolen from our nation and families! It's time for the Church to shine with the light of Jesus! It's time that God's people arise and declare war on the enemy! It's time to penetrate every sphere of society and take it over for King Jesus: the government, the education system, the arts, the medical world, the mass media, the financial institutions! Let's tell the enemy: Thus far and no more! Get out in Jesus' name!

LORD, SHOW ME MY WEAPONS!

> "....for the weapons of our warfare are not worldly but have divine power to destroy strongholds." (2 Corinthians 10:4).

Just like David, we have five "stones" that we carry with us at all times (1 Samuel 17: 40). Because we love Jesus and we love people, we want to see people and nations saved, healed, delivered, restored. These are the main weapons we have "at hand":

1. The Holy Spirit!

> "...for he who is in you is greater than he who is in the world." (1 John 4:4).

The Lord has not sent us to battle without equipping us; He has gifted us with Himself! The Holy Spirit gifts us with very powerful gifts (1 Corinthians 12: 4-11) to destroy the works of the enemy and to set the captives free from all kinds of misery: sickness, disease, evil spirits, ignorance, depression, addictions, confusion, lies. This is why the entire Church needs to be baptized in the Holy Spirit, just like Jesus and the early Church! In addition we have the seven-fold manifestation of the Holy Spirit working in our lives: the Spirit of the Lord, spirit of wisdom and understanding, the spirit of counsel and might, the spirit of knowledge and the fear of the Lord (Isaiah 11:2).

Pentecost is not just a historical event, but it is meant to be experienced by every believer! This is God's plan to have a healthy, strong, vibrant Church! This is why Jesus made sure that His followers would not leave Jerusalem until they received the promise of the Father: the Holy Spirit! Without the power of the Holy Spirit we do not have weapons to fight and overcome the enemy! Without the Holy Spirit we cannot defend ourselves from the attacks of the enemy!

Last month in Kotido, Uganda, we went to pray for the sick at its health center before moving on to the next assignment. We went and ministered healing to two patients that were lying in bed looking almost dead. As we moved on to the next "patient," suddenly the wailing of a woman was heard. The screams were becoming louder and louder; it was a young mother crying and shouting that her baby was dying! The baby's body was limp, and foam was coming out of her mouth. The baby was motionless. I knew this was a divine appointment! Immediately we took authority in the name of Jesus over the spirit of death that was trying to kill her baby and commanded it to leave. We laid hands and released the healing of the kingdom of God on this baby; we proclaimed life and healing on her. The Holy Spirit showed me that this baby was wearing objects of witchcraft; therefore they needed to be removed in order for the healing to flow. The translator told the mother to remove any articles of witchcraft from the baby, because they could hinder the healing from taking place. Immediately the mother broke off with her teeth those fetishes from the baby's body. As I looked around the room, the man we had previously laid hands on was seating and getting ready to get out of bed to eat; the other lady was already sitting on her bed with a different look on her face. The baby was healed and by the time we left she was being bathed!

Brothers and sisters, we have been equipped to destroy every yoke of bondage, sickness and disease through the anointing of the Holy Spirit! We have been equipped with revelatory gifts that give great glory to God as we build up His Kingdom. We have access to the invisible realm through the Holy Spirit. As kingdom people, this is how we extend His kingdom on earth as it is in heaven! It's a matter of stepping out in faith to carry on with the works of Jesus! We are alive for this purpose!

2. The Blood of Jesus!

> "And they have conquered him by the blood of the Lamb and by the word of their testimony…."
> (Revelation 12:11).

Our victory is the precious blood of Jesus! We have to know the power of the blood of Jesus, remind ourselves at all times what He has done for us and proclaim it with our mouths:

Every and any claim the enemy could have against us is wiped away by the precious blood of the Lamb! (Hebrews 9:22; Ephesians 1:7).

John says:

"...and the blood of Jesus His Son cleanses us from all sin." (1 John 1:7).

We have been redeemed by the blood of Jesus (Ephesians 1:7). In other words, we have been bought out of the hand of the devil at a price: the blood of Jesus! Peter says:

"You know that you were ransomed from the futile ways inherited from your fathers, not with perishable things such as silver or gold, but with the precious blood of Christ...." (1 Peter 1:18-19).

Reconciliation and peace with the Lord is ours because of the blood of the Lamb. (Colossians 1:20).

"Therefore, since we are justified by faith, we have peace with God through our Lord Jesus Christ." (Romans 5:1).

Justification is ours by the blood of the Lamb. (Romans 3:22-25).

"Since therefore, we are now justified by his blood...." (Romans 5:9).

"Sanctification is ours through the blood of the Lamb." Hebrews 13:12 says,

"So Jesus also suffered outside the gate in order to sanctify the people through his own blood."

We have access to the throne of God through the blood of

Jesus. Hebrews 9:12 says,

> "...he entered once for all into the Holy Place, taking not the blood of goats and calves but his own blood, thus securing an eternal redemption."

Protection is ours in the blood of Jesus. We must learn to "apply" the blood of Jesus over every area of our lives for protection from the enemy. Just as God's people on the night of the Passover were protected because they applied the blood of the lamb over the doorposts of their houses, we must learn to live under the protection of the blood of Jesus (Exodus 12:22-23). This is not a meditation about the blood of the Lamb, but a spoken testimony, a proclamation of what the blood of Jesus has done for us! The blood of Jesus is more powerful than any demonic assignment released against us; therefore, appropriate it!

Next time you go to Mass, celebrate the Blood of Jesus as the priest lifts up the cup of our redemption! Thank Him for your redemption, your forgiveness, your justification, your sanctification, your protection! This is our reality!

3. The Word of God!

> "...the sword of the Spirit, which is the word of God." (Ephesians 6:17).

The Word of God is an offensive weapon in our mouths; just like Jesus when He was tempted in the wilderness, we need to "wield" our swords to defeat the enemy. It's tragic to see so many of God's people not be in the Word of God; therefore they are swordless! On the "evil day" (Ephesians 6:13) they have no swords to wield against the enemy!

When the Holy Spirit "quickens" the written Word of God in the Bible, He is speaking directly to you and you better listen! He is giving you a "sword" for you to wield! Memorize that passage; it will come handy at just the right time.

I love the story of one of David's mighty men, Eleazar the son of Dodo. Look at what it says about him in 2 Samuel 23:10:

> "He rose and struck down the Philistines until his hand was weary, and his hand cleaved to the sword; and the Lord wrought a great victory that day...."

We need to "cleave" our hand to the Word of God until we see victory!

As a single mother one "sword" that I clung to and wielded many, many times was Psalm 37:25,

> "I have been young, and now am old; yet I have not seen the righteous forsaken or his children begging bread."

You see, after my marriage broke, the enemy kept tormenting me with lies such as "Your children will never amount to anything now"; "your children will never move forward in life;" "your children will never be healed." One day I was in my kitchen reading Psalm 37, and when I got to verse 25, the Holy Spirit quickened that verse. Faith rose up in me and I boldly declared what the Bible was saying; I told the enemy "You are a liar and what I believe is what the Word of God says: my children will never beg for bread! Get out in Jesus' name!" Suddenly I experienced victory and freedom from the liar! The Lord was teaching me how to wield my "sword" and experience victory! The Holy Spirit is the One that trains our hands for war and our fingers for battle! (Psalm 144:1).

Today I can boldly shout from the rooftop that God is FAITHFUL and the enemy is a LIAR!

My four children have moved forward in life and continue to do so! Alleluia!

Several years ago in Uganda, I was praying in the Spirit on my way to Kabale region, and I heard the voice of God tell me this:

"The edges of My Sword are detestable to the devil."

This is what the Holy Spirit showed me:

The devil hates the Word of God! The edges of His Sword are truth and light:

The Word of God is truth; since the enemy is a liar (John 8:44), he hates the truth of the Word of God!

Truth dispels the lies within the demonic strongholds in our minds; as those "walls" come tumbling down, we enter into more freedom!

The Word of God releases light (Psalm 119:105-130); since the enemy functions in darkness, he hates the light! Light is more powerful than darkness; once we "see" he has no more power over us!

The "sword of the Spirit" releases truth and light into the lies, deception and darkness of the enemy, and he is uncovered!

Many Catholics have believed the lie that the Word of God is not that important; therefore they don't take the time to read, study or meditate on the Scriptures. This lie comes from the pit of hell! This is a major reason why we see the Catholic Church at this time so weak and asleep! I say it's time to wake up!

> "Awake, O sleeper, and arise from the dead, and Christ shall give you light" (Ephesians 5:14).

4. Praise and Worship

> "Let the high praises of God be in their throats and
>   two-edged swords in their hands,
> To wreak vengeance on the nations and chastisement on
>   the peoples,
> To bind their kings with chains and their nobles with
>   fetters of iron,
> To execute on them the judgment written!
> This is glory for all his faithful ones. Praise the Lord!"
> (Psalm 149:6-9).

The high praises of God not only defeat the enemy but shame him! It is our glory that through our praises of Jesus we "bind" and "execute" judgment on the enemy! We shout, sing, clap, dance, twirl, jump and heaven invades earth! When heaven invades earth the enemy can't stay!

> "Let God arise, let His enemies be scattered!"
> (Psalm 68:1).

Praise is a weapon of warfare! It shatters the plans and the strongholds of the enemy. In 2 Chronicles 20:1-30, we see that as God's people praised the Lord, not only was the enemy confused and defeated, but God's people were able to take over the spoils of the enemy. In Acts 16, as Paul and Silas praised the Lord in prison, there was an earthquake that caused doors to open and chains to break, releasing deliverance and salvation!

We praise the Lord because He is worthy of all our praise. No matter what we're going through, He deserves our praise at all times. Especially during difficult times, I have learned that "the harder the place, the bigger the praise!" We cannot allow our senses and emotions to control us! We must live with a kingdom mentality at all times, knowing that King Jesus is on the throne. As temples of the Holy Spirit, we must learn how to create an atmosphere in our lives where the Holy Spirit can thrive. Praise and worship are the atmosphere of heaven, and as we praise the Lord with the high praises the kingdom of God is released! The Lord inhabits the praises of His people (Psalm 22:3) and mighty things happen; the atmosphere changes and breakthroughs are released! Healings, miracles, revelation, restoration, joy, victory becomes a reality in His presence!

During a WOW conference in Lira, Uganda, last month, the Holy Spirit moved in great power as God's people praised and worshiped the Lord. I will mention a few testimonies of captives being set free:

A lady suffering for fifty-one years of pain in her uterus was totally set free! She jumped up and down, full of joy and gladness, giving glory to the Lord!

A lady suffering for twenty-one years from a skin disorder was healed through a word of knowledge. The bumps and itching on her skin totally disappeared and her skin became smooth and nice.

A lady suffering from multiple pains and swelling in her body causing her to walk crooked was healed and set free from pain. She jumped with all her might and walked just fine!

An older lady who came to the conference totally depressed, angry and bitter was set free. She was angry that her son, who was a priest, had died nine years ago. She was angry with God, with the world, with life; she was joyless. As we ministered together with the worship team from Song of Solomon, the Holy Spirit just hovered over her and she experienced the love of Jesus and was set free from the anger and depression! She looked as if she had received a "face lift!" The glory of God was all over her face!

This is what is happening all over the world as His people praise and worship Him in "spirit and it truth."

It's important that we become worshipers of God; if we are not worshiping God, we are worshiping something else. Ultimately, we become a slave of whatever/whoever we worship! Why not worship Jesus with all your heart?

> "But the hour is coming, and now is, when the true worshippers will worship the Father in spirit and truth, for such the Father seeks to worship him. God is spirit, and those who worship him must worship in spirit and truth." (John 4:23-24).

5. Prayer

> "Happy is the man who listens to me, watching daily at
> my gates, waiting beside my doors.
> For he who finds me finds life and obtains favor from the
> Lord...." (Proverbs 8:24-25).

Prayer is the foundation of our walk with the Lord. This is how we build a relationship with Him: by meeting Him daily, spending time with Him and with the Scriptures, hearing His voice, being a doer of the Word. The time spent with the Lord in our prayer closet is invaluable. I believe that as we spend time with the Lord we are actually storing treasure in our heavenly bank accounts, and as the need arises we can "withdraw" what is needed at the right time!

According to the above passage from the Scriptures, we must listen to the Lord. Listening involves watching and waiting! It's not the quick, "in and out," fast-paced mentality that we learned in the world! It involves patience. In the Spirit realm there are "gates" and "doors" just like in the physical world; it's there that we position ourselves as we pray. It's in the "gates" that we find wisdom:

> "...on the top of the walls she cries out; at the entrance of the city gates she speaks...." (Proverbs 1:21).

> "...beside the gates in front of the town, at the entrance of the portals she cries aloud...." (Proverbs 8:3).

David said,

> "But for me it is good to be near God...." (Psalm 73:28).

Intimacy with the Lord in prayer is the key to abiding in Him. As we remain abiding in Him, we experience His presence at all times; in the flow of His Spirit we have life and His favor is released upon us! It is His favor that opens doors for us and this favor is ours!

> "...and those who rise early to see him will find favor." (Sirach 32:14b).

In 1 Samuel 22, David is facing another crisis and he asks the king of Moab if his parents can stay with him

> "until I know what God will do for me." (v.3).

David had a confidence in God that was truly amazing! He knew that it was God Who had chosen him and anointed him to be the next king of Israel; therefore David knew that the Lord Himself would do whatever was necessary so that David could fulfill his purpose and God-ordained destiny. David says in Psalm 57:2,

> "I cry to God Most High, to God who fulfills his purpose for me."

David says in Psalm 138:8,

> "The Lord will fulfill his purpose for me…."

Do you have that assurance, that certainty, that the Lord is totally committed to fulfill His purpose and calling on your life? Like the Apostle Paul we can say:

> "And I am sure that he who began a good work in you will bring it to completion…." (Philippians 1:6).

It was a pattern in David's life to turn to the Lord with confidence and to inquire of Him. This should become our pattern in this life. Let's make the "prayer" of Habakkuk ours:

> "I will take my stand to watch, and station myself on the tower, and look forth to see what he will say to me…." (Habakkuk 2:1).

The way has been opened to us through the blood of Jesus to go before the throne of grace with boldness and ask our God for whatever we need (Hebrews 4:16). This access we have always and everywhere!

Like David, we should get to the point in our relationship with the Lord that we can say from the heart,

> "O Lord, I love the habitation of thy house, and the place where thy glory dwells." (Psalm 26:8).

V

"THE LUST OF THE EYES"

> "Do not love the world or the things in the world. If any one loves the world, love for the Father is not in him. For all that is in the world, the lust of the flesh and the lust of the eyes and the pride of life, is not of the Father but is of the world. (John 2:15-16).

The eye gate is a battlefield; there are invisible forces trying to get control of it. As God's people and temples of the Holy Spirit, we need to be aware that our eyes are an entry point for good and evil, light and darkness, and we need to protect this gate from the enemy's temptations, tactics and snares. It's our responsibility to keep our "temples" guarded and protected from the enemy. We need to honor the Holy Spirit and treasure His presence.

In Genesis 3, the story of man's downfall, the eyes played a crucial role in that disaster. The serpent, being very cunning, started sowing lies into Eve regarding what God had said. This created doubt and confusion in Eve; good soil for disobedience. As the devil tempted Eve to eat of the forbidden fruit from the tree of the knowledge of good and evil, there was a contest for her eyes. Let's read:

> "But the serpent said to the woman, You will not die. For God knows that when you eat of it your eyes will be opened and you will be like God, knowing good and evil. So when the woman saw that the tree was good for food, and that it was a delight to the eyes, and that the tree was to be desired to make one wise, she took of its fruit and

> ate; and she also gave some to her husband, and he ate. Then the eyes of both were opened…." (Genesis 3:5-7).

According to satan, the biggest "benefit" of eating of the forbidden fruit was to have their eyes opened so that they could be "like God, knowing good and evil." That was the bait! That was "the carrot on the stick!" Obedience to God's Word became unimportant at that moment; the forbidden fruit of the tree of the knowledge of good and evil became more and more appealing to Eve as she continued to "look" and delight herself in what she saw with her eyes.

> "Then the eyes of both were opened, and they knew that they were naked; and they sewed fig leaves together and made themselves aprons." (v.7).

They lost their innocence through their disobedience, but most importantly, because they ate from the tree of the knowledge of good and evil, they ate its fruit: death. Demonic seeds of death and sin entered humanity: pride, rebellion, disobedience, depression, addictions, sexual immorality, spiritual deafness and blindness, poverty, fear, anxiety, shame, sickness, etc. They acted independently of God and became conscious of "self;" shame and fear replaced the joy and intimacy they once enjoyed with the Lord. Their wrong choice was influenced by looking at the fruit from the forbidden tree. The enemy used their eye gate as the point of entry to tempt them and disobey God. For Eve the forbidden fruit became a delight to her eyes as she kept focusing on it.

I want to make a point regarding Eve and I am not excusing her for disobeying God. She communed with God in the garden, but she didn't receive first-hand revelation from God regarding the tree of the knowledge of good and evil. The Lord gave the instructions directly to Adam (Genesis 2:16-17) and Adam passed it on to Eve. Brothers and sisters, it's important that each individual receive revelation and vision personally. It is not enough at times (especially on the "evil day") to live on second-hand revelation or information. All of us have a specific plan and purpose from the Lord and we must hear from Him personally so that His Words really become alive in us.

It will be worth the while to meditate on the story of man's fall from grace; the enemy has not changed his tactics! He's contending for our eye gate! He tried to seduce Jesus through His eye gate as well! While Jesus was being tempted in the desert, one of the temptations involved His eyes:

> "Again, the devil took him to a very high mountain, and showed him all the kingdoms of the world and the glory of them; and he said to him, 'All these I will give you, if you will fall down and worship me.'" (Matthew 4:8-9).

Jesus overcame that temptation, quoting from the Scriptures, for He knew Who He was, He knew what His mission was, and He knew that all the kingdoms would be His after His death and resurrection. As it says in Revelation 11: 15,

> "The kingdom of the world has become the kingdom of our Lord and of his Christ, and he shall reign for ever and ever."

Job made a covenant with his eyes:

> "I have made a covenant with my eyes;
> How then could I look upon a virgin?" (Job 31:1).

What are the "virgins" in your life? Identify them and make a commitment, just like Job, not to look at them any longer. God's grace is more powerful than your weakness! (2 Corinthians 12:9). Let's desire to be filled with God's light and not with darkness. It's time for God's people to make a covenant with our eyes, to look only at Him, His Word, His promises; to see dreams and visions; to look at what He is doing today, to see from His perspective, so that we will not miss His plans and purposes for these times. We cannot use our eyes in the wrong ways and expect God to show us great and hidden things in the Spirit realm.

Psalm 101:3 says,

> "I will not set before my eyes anything that is base."

Proverbs 23:26,

> "My child, pay attention to me, let your eyes take pleasure in my way."

Let's start listening to the Lord and taking delight in His ways instead! It's our choice!

Proverbs 4:25-27:

> "Let your eyes look directly forward, and your gaze be straight before you.
> Take heed to the path of your feet, then all your ways will be sure.
> Do not swerve to the right or to the left; turn your foot away from evil."

Let's keep our eyes on the goal, not being distracted by what the world offers or by other people's opinions.

> "...let us run with perseverance the race that is set before us, looking to Jesus the pioneer and perfecter of our faith...."

Keeping our eyes on Jesus, our great reward, will get us to get to our destiny!

In Ezekiel 20:7, the Lord speaks through the prophet:

> "And I said to them, cast away the detestable things your eyes feast on, every one of you, and do not defile yourselves with the idols of Egypt; I am the Lord your God. But they rebelled against me and would not listen to me; they did not every man cast away the detestable things their eyes feasted on, nor did they forsake the idols of Egypt."

Are your eyes "feasting" on the wrong things?

Today pornography is an epidemic, not only in the world, but inside the church! Believe me, I have prayed with countless church people of every age, sex and race for deliverance from this demon. They started peeking into it and before they knew it they were controlled by it, and now they cannot get away from it. Why do I mention this? Because when we use our eyes for the wrong things, how can we expect the Lord to trust us with more revelation, dreams and visions? When we open the gates of our eyes to the enemy by the wrong use of our eyes, darkness comes into us! Then we wonder why God is not speaking, why we feel depressed, discouraged and downtrodden! Guess what? Your eye gate might be the problem!

"...and never satisfied are the eyes of man."
(Proverbs 27:20).

Another "epidemic" we are facing today is the rise of occultism in many different forms. When we engage in occultism, be assured that darkness is what will come inside us. It's an open door for the enemy to "steal, kill and destroy" in your life. Psychic hotlines, horoscopes, New Age, Ouija boards, mediums, witchcraft, Santeria, voodoo, channeling, palm-reading, etc. are detestable to the Lord and give "legal" access to the enemy to harass and torment us! (Deuteronomy 18:9-12). Sickness, disease, mental illness, depression, confusion, etc. , are some of the "fruit" of occultism. Can we expect the Lord to release to us a download of revelation and share His secrets with us if we are receiving revelation from another source? Our God is a "jealous" God! (Exodus 20:5). He will not tolerate our rebellion and disobedience. Can we even expect to walk in victory and experience the abundant life when we have open doors to the enemy? In the Cuban-American culture, for example, it is very common for Catholics to attend Mass on Sundays and engage in Santeria (Cuban witchcraft) the rest of the week. In their ignorance they want to "cover all the bases." This unholy "mixture" of the holy with the demonic will keep us bound and blind; our descendants will suffer the consequences as well! What kind of a spiritual inheritance are you leaving your children and your children's children?

VI

THE EYES: THE DOWNFALL OF MANY

"If your right eye causes you to sin, pluck it out and throw it away…." (Matthew 5:29).

There are many examples of God's people in the Bible where their eyes played a crucial role in their downfalls. Let's examine some of them and ask the Lord to speak to us and show us where or if we need to make any adjustments in the way we have been using our eyes.

CAIN: Self-centeredness; rebellion; disobedience

Let's look at Cain. Cain is the prototype of the self-centered person who wants to do things "his" way; and when things don't turn out his way, anger sets in. Cain had a problem with spiritual blindness; he could not "see" which kind of offering pleased the Lord. His brother Abel brought to the Lord the offerings that pleased Him. Cain brought to the Lord what Cain thought was okay, which wasn't. (It's implied that the Lord gave to both of them the revelation of the offerings that pleased Him). The Lord showed His pleasure with Abel's offerings, but not with Cain's (Genesis 4: 4-5). Cain "was very angry, and his countenance fell" (v.5). What was going on here? I believe there was a big root of rebellion, defiance and disobedience in Cain, which blinded him to truth and made him very stubborn. Sin has a blinding effect. Look at what the prophet Obadiah says,

> "The pride of your heart has deceived you...."
> (Obadiah v.3).

If our hearts are not right with God, being involved in religious activity will not touch His heart. Look at Amos 5:22-23:

> "I hate, I despise your feasts, and I take no delight in
> your solemn assemblies.
> Even though you offer me your burnt offerings and
> cereal offerings, I will not accept them,
> And the peace offerings of your fatted beasts I will not
> look upon.
> Take away from me the noise of your songs; to the
> melody of your harps I will not listen.
> But let justice roll down like waters, and righteousness
> like an ever-flowing stream."

The Lord in His mercy reached down to Cain and said to him:

> "Why are you angry, and why has your countenance
> fallen? If you do well, will you not be accepted?
> And if you do not do well, sin is crouching at the door;
> its desire is for you, but you must master it." (v.6-7).

Even after the Lord mercifully reached down to Cain trying to put some God-sense into him, Cain disregarded it and ended up killing his brother Abel. (Genesis 4:8). Cain's uncontrolled anger led him to murder. After Cain murdered Abel, God asked him where Abel was and this is Cain's response:

> "I do not know; am I my brother's keeper?" (v.9).

Cain lied and showed no repentance! His heart was hardened with no sensitivity towards God nor others.

Now, you could be telling yourself, this doesn't apply to me. My question for you is this: Are you a doer of God's Word, or are you a doer of 50%of God's Word? 60%? 85%? Obedience is not complete obedience unless its 100% obedience! Are you involved in religious activities that the Lord has not asked you to be involved in? Are you living in a way that pleases God, or is there compromise with sin in your life? Are there areas of stubbornness in your life where you are doing things "your" way and not God's way? Do you downplay your lies calling them "white lies?" Are you feeding yourself from the Scriptures, knowing that they are God's standards, or you show little interest for the Word of God? Cain brought offerings to the Lord, but the wrong kind of offerings. Are you giving the Lord the best of your tithes and offerings, or are you just "tipping" Him with your leftovers?

LOT:
lack of vision; double-mindedness;
indifference and complacency.

Lot, Abraham's nephew, represents the kind of person that is lukewarm and double-minded, who chooses what looks good to the natural eye, instead of inquiring of the Lord and trying to see from God's perspective. He is the kind of person who has no wisdom and no vision for the future, but is carnal-minded, self-pleasing rather than a God pleaser! Paul says in Romans 8:8,

"…and those who are in the flesh cannot please God."

In my opinion, Lot was just tagging along with Abraham, without a deep conviction and revelation of God's plans and purposes. He just went along for the ride! Like Eve, he really didn't have a vision or revelation of his own. He reminds me of Esau, Jacob's brother, who sold his birthright for a bowl of lentils (Genesis 25:29-34). Proverbs 29:18 says,

"Where there is no vision the people get out of hand…." (NJB)

It's easy to "get out of hand," demoralized, unrestrained when there is no vision or personal revelation from the Lord. When the time came for Abraham and Lot to separate (Genesis 13:5-11), Abraham gave Lot the opportunity to choose first what land he would settle in. Lot looked around and made his choice:

> "And Lot lifted up his eyes, and saw that the Jordan valley was well watered everywhere like the garden of the Lord, like the land of Egypt, in the direction of Zoar; this was before the Lord destroyed Sodom and Gomorrah. So Lot chose for himself all the Jordan valley, and Lot journeyed east; thus they separated from each other." (Genesis 13:10-11).

Lot chose the area of Sodom and Gomorrah to settle in and raise a family. This was not a good choice! He definitely did not have a "good" eye! His double-mindedness kept him unsteady. God said this of Sodom:

> "Now the men of Sodom were wicked, great sinners against the Lord." (Genesis 13:13).

Lot chose the worst possible place to make his home in; a place full of depravity and sin! No wisdom there. He based his decision just on what he saw with his natural eyes: he liked what he saw and he wanted it. He saw the "prosperity" of the place and his focus was not on the Lord, but on a comfortable and easy life, with tons of opportunities to move up the corporate ladder! This shows his double-mindedness: he wanted what the world had to offer, disregarding what God had to say about it. John says in John 2:15-16,

> "Do not love the world or the things in the world. If anyone loves the world, love for the Father is not in him. For all that is in the world, the lust of the flesh and the lust of the eyes and the pride of life, is not of the Father but is of the world."

At the end of his story, when the Lord finally decides to destroy Sodom and Gomorrah because of its wickedness, we see that Lot finally had to run away from Sodom in order to save his life, leaving behind all his material wealth and everything that he had worked for! His life was saved, period. All his wealth lost, in the twinkling of an eye! Paul says in 1 Corinthians 3:

> "For no other foundation can any one lay than that which is laid, which is Jesus Christ. Now if any one builds on the foundation with gold, silver, precious stones, wood, hay, stubble—each man's work will become manifest; for the Day will disclose it, because it will be revealed with fire, and the fire will test what sort of work each one has done. If the work which any man has built on the foundation survives, he will receive a reward. If any man's work is burned up, he will suffer loss, though he himself will be saved, but only as through fire."

The fruit of Lot's life was not good: he became the father of the Moabites and the Ammonites, both enemies of Israel! (Genesis 19:37-38). Bad choices: bad fruit!

Ask yourself: Do I have a vision of my own, or am I just going along with second-hand revelation? How am I making my choices? Am I making them according to what my natural eyes see, or do I turn to the Holy Spirit and the Scriptures for guidance? Do I try to see things from God's perspective in order to make the choice that pleases Him, or do I make my choices based on what I want at the moment, with no consideration of consequences? Do I realize that my choices of today will affect my family for generations to come?

> "He who finds his life will lose it, and he who loses his life for my sake will find it." (Matthew 10:39).

LOT'S WIFE:
Unbelief; lack of vision; stuck in the past.

Lot's wife stands for the Church person who has no relationship with the Lord and no faith, even though he/she sits on the pews of the Church and has been exposed to the things of God. She walked by sight and not by faith, just the opposite of how we are supposed to walk on this planet (2 Corinthians 5:7). Like her husband Lot, she was really in love with the things of the world. Her spiritual life had never taken off. When they had to finally leave Sodom behind because the Lord was getting ready to destroy it, the angels gave them specific instructions:

> "Flee for your life; do not look back or stop anywhere in the valley, flee to the hills, lest you be consumed." (Genesis 19:17).

What did Lot's wife do?

> "But Lot's wife behind him looked back, and she became a pillar of salt." (v.26).

Lot's wife's left her heart in Sodom, that place where she had lived in great comfort and complacency, even though it was full of sexual immorality and perversion. Those things had never seemed to bother her; "to each their own" was her attitude. She was even more attached to Sodom that her husband Lot. She could not conceive of life after Sodom. She had "no" spiritual vision! As she turned to look at Sodom, she probably lingered, wishing in her heart to be back there as in former days; whatever exploded in Sodom covered her and that was that. Brothers and sisters, we can't live in the past! If we are stuck in the past, we can't move into our destiny! Isaiah says,

> "Behold, I am doing a new thing; now it springs forth,
> do you not perceive it?
> I will make a way in the wilderness and rivers in the
> desert." (Isaiah 43:19).

Lot's wife had never had the eyes of her heart opened; she never cared about God's Word and because of her ignorance of the Scriptures she never could walk by faith. At the moment of crisis, she had no faith and could not conceive that the Lord could take care of them after Sodom's destruction. No faith, no hope, no revelation! She had no faith, because she had made no time to listen to the Word of the Lord (Romans 10:17). If Lot didn't make it with "second-hand revelation", Lot's wife had third-hand revelation! She never took the time to search whatever truth she had received from her husband. The Scriptures say,

> "Remember Lot's wife." (Luke 17:32).

Jesus said,

> "No one who puts his hand to the plow and looks back is fit for the kingdom of God." (Luke 9:62).

My question for you is this: How are you spending your free time? Are you sinking your roots deeper and deeper into God's Word, or are you spending your time reading worldly, secular material that will not transform your mind nor help you to walk by faith? How are you keeping your mind renewed, day by day? Is your past holding you in bondage, or are you living in the freedom of a child of God? Is there hunger in your heart to know God and know His promises? What are you doing about it? Jesus said that only when we build our house on the rock of His Word, our house will not fall:

> "Every one then who hears these words of mine and does them will be like a wise man who built his house upon the rock; and the rain fell, and the floods came, and the winds blew and beat upon that house, but it did not fall, because it had been founded on the rock. And every one who hears these words of mine and does not do them will be like a foolish man who build his house upon the sand; and the rain fell and the floods came, and the winds blew and beat against that house, and it fell; and great was the fall of it." (Matthew 7:24-27).

Are you building your house on the rock or on the sand?

AN ENTIRE ISRAELITE GENERATION
(Except for Joshua and Caleb): unbelief; wrong perspective; grasshopper complex; negativity.

> "...and we seemed to ourselves like grasshoppers, and so we seemed to them." (Numbers 13:33).

It's all about perspective! It is absolutely tragic what happened to the Israelites in the wilderness: Because of their unbelief and wrong perspective, God could do only half of what He had planned to do for them. God was able to take them out of Egypt, but He was not able to take them into the Promised Land, even though this was God's perfect will and plan for their lives! They still had a slave mentality and were unable to see themselves in the light of God's revealed truth: as God's covenant people to whom God was committed to fulfill His promise and plan to give them a land of their own.

Ten of the twelve spies whom Moses sent to spy out the Promised Land came back with a "negative report" that spread like wildfire among God's people:

> "Yet the people who dwell in the land are strong, and the cities are fortified and very large; and besides we saw the descendants of Anak there.... We are not able to go up against the people; for they are stronger than we. So they brought to the people of Israel an evil report of the land which they had spied out, saying, The land...is a land that devours its inhabitants; and all the people that we saw in it are men of great stature...and we seemed like grasshoppers, and so we seemed to them." (Numbers 13:28-33).

The "grasshopper" mentality will never usher you into your destiny! What is the grasshopper mentality?

It's thinking "I can't do it!" "I'm not gifted!" "I'm not strong enough!" "I'm not good enough!" and so on. The Lord tells you to prophesy, and you don't because you are afraid it might "not be God"; the Lord tells you to lay hands on the sick, and you don't because you are afraid they might not get healed; the Lord asks you share the gospel and you don't because you are afraid of rejection. Excuses, excuses, excuses! Many in the Church are suffering from the "grasshopper complex!" I say it's grasshopper-crushing time!

Only two spies, Joshua and Caleb, believed that God was able to fulfill what He had promised: to bring them into a land flowing with milk and honey. Caleb said,

> "...Let us go up at once, and occupy it; for we are well able to overcome it." (Numbers 13:30).

In Numbers 14:9 Caleb said,

> "Only do not rebel against the Lord; and do not fear the people of the land, for they are bread for us; their protection is removed from them, and the Lord is with us; do not fear them."

Joshua and Caleb believed God; they put their trust on God's word and the fact that if God was with them, nothing could stop them from possessing the land. They focused on the promise; they had the correct perspective. The rest of the people focused on the problem, forgot about God's promise and were gripped with unbelief!

Focusing on the problem and circumstances releases fear! Focusing on God's promises releases faith!

Ask yourself: Which "camp" do I belong to? Joshua's and Caleb's? Or the ten other spies'? Are there "grasshoppers" in my thinking? What am I focusing on? The problem or the promise? What comes out of my mouth? Words of faith, or negativity, doubt, unbelief, grumbling complaining? Has the Lord been able to fulfill and accomplish His will and plan for my life, or only half?

ACHAN:
lust of the eyes; roots of greed and avarice.

Achan's story is found in Joshua 7. It is kind of a shocking story because in Achan's background there was no trace that he would do something like what he did: he stole what belonged to the Lord. People would say that what Achan did was "unexpected." Achan never stood out one way or another. When God's army invaded and conquered Jericho, Achan fixed his eyes on what was forbidden. He probably thought to himself "I deserve this; I fought long and hard."

> "Remember that a greedy eye is a bad thing. What has been created more greedy than the eye?" (Sirach 31:13).

Achan was one of the Israelites who survived the desert experience; as he walked through the desert his clothes and shoes never wore out nor did he ever get sick (Nehemiah 9:21); he ate manna in the desert and drank water from the rock; he was there when Joshua became leader; he crossed over the Jordan River miraculously; he circumcised himself with the rest of the men before taking over the Promised Land; he was there fighting for Jericho. What I'm trying to say is that he experienced the signs and wonders and did what was required of him. We don't see a trace of rebellion and disobedience until Jericho is taken over. In the same way, there are many people in church today who participate in religious activities, but the reality of the gospel has not penetrated deep enough into their hearts. They go to church because it's the thing to do, but no real commitment to the Lord; when temptation comes, they are not strong enough to resist the devil.

Joshua warned the Israelites and gave clear instructions regarding the spoils of war; it all belonged to the Lord:

> "But you, keep yourselves from the things devoted to destruction, lest when you have devoted them you take any of the devoted things and make the camp of Israel a thing for destruction, and bring trouble upon it. But all the silver and gold, and vessels of bronze and iron, are sacred to the Lord; they shall go into the treasury of the Lord." (Joshua 6:18-19).

Achan disobeyed Joshua's instructions; I imagine that as he stole what belonged to the Lord, he was thinking that no one would find out. Indeed, no human being found out, but God did! There were major consequences for the nation of Israel because of Achan's sin: they were miserably defeated when they proceeded to take over the next city, Ai, a less fortified city than Jericho. Joshua was beside himself, not understanding the reason why they were defeated in Ai. The Lord then spoke to him:

> "Israel has sinned; they have transgressed my covenant which I commanded them; they have taken some of the devoted things; they have stolen and lied, and put them among their own stuff." (Joshua 7:11).

Eventually, Achan was found out and confessed:

> "…when I saw among the spoils a beautiful mantle from Shinar, and two hundred shekels of silver, and a bar of gold weighing fifty shekels, then I coveted them, and took them…." (Joshua 7:21).

Achan's eyes got him into trouble; he coveted the silver and the gold and the beautiful mantle. He had never been exposed to those things before and could not resist the temptation to steal them and have a secure future for him and his family. His retirement was taken care of! Surely, who would ever find out what he did? The owner of these things was dead!

Achan and his family were stoned to death and with all his belongings burned with fire.

Achan looked good and smelled good, but his heart was not totally submitted to the Lord. There was hidden greed in his heart. He reminds me of believers who never look inside their hearts to see what is hidden there, so hidden sin and iniquity are never dealt with. The name Achan means serpent, vexation; trouble. Indeed he was sneaky as a serpent, lying low and quiet, waiting for a good opportunity to take what didn't belong to him. He didn't care about consequences as long as he got what his eyes coveted. After all, he fought hard in Jericho; in his twisted way of thinking, he deserved those things!

My question for you is this: how has the Gospel changed

your life? How deeply has it penetrated your heart? Have you searched your heart and asked the Lord to show you anything that is hidden and displeasing in His sight? David said,

> "But who can discern his errors? Clear thou me from
> hidden faults.
> Keep back thy servant also from presumptuous sins;
> let them not have dominion over!
> Then I shall be blameless, and innocent of great
> transgression." (Psalm 19:12-13).

Ask the Holy Spirit to show you any hidden and displeasing areas of your life that you are not aware of, so that you can repent and be transformed! Pluck out those roots of greed and covetousness!

SAMSON:
lust of the eyes; sexual immorality.

Samson stands for the Christian who is very gifted but keeps setting his mind on the things of the flesh (Romans 8:6). Samson had a great destiny that was only partially fulfilled because his eyes kept getting him into trouble. We find Samson's story in Judges 13-16. He had a "weakness" for women:

> "Samson went down to Timnah, and at Timnah he saw one of the daughters of the Philistines. Then he came up, and told his father and mother, I saw one of the daughters of the Philistines at Timnah; now get her for me as my wife. But his father and mother said to him, 'Is there not a woman among daughters of your kinsmen, or among all our people, that you must go to take a wife from the uncircumcised Philistines?' But Samson said to his father, 'Get her for me; for she pleases me well.'" (Judges 14:1-3).

What Samson saw, Samson wanted! He wanted a Philistine woman, even though the Lord specifically said not to intermarry with them. He wanted what pleased his eye. Again in Judges 16:1 we see the same pattern:

> "Samson went to Gaza, and there he saw a harlot, and he went in to her."

Judges 16:4 says,

> "After this he loved a woman in the valley of Sorek, whose name was Delilah."

We could say that Samson needed deliverance from a spirit of sexual immorality! His conception and birth amazing (Judges 13); consecrated to the Lord from the womb, destined to be a great deliverer for Israel, he messed up his life because of the lusts of the eyes and flesh. Maybe Samson used his imagination in the wrong way, thinking of his next sexual encounter, instead of thinking of things above; as he engaged the eyes of his heart to think about the wrong things, more and more darkness entered in. Does this happen still today? You bet! Samson went from woman to woman until he met Delilah, who betrayed him to the Philistines for 11 hundred pieces of silver. The name "Delilah" comes from a root that means "to be brought low." She brought Samson low indeed! Watch out for the company you keep!

Delilah pressured Samson to tell her the secret of his strength, and when he did,

> "She made him sleep upon her knees; and she called a man, and had him shave off the seven locks of his head. Then she began to torment him and his strength left him. And she said, The Philistines are upon you, Samson! And he awoke from his sleep, and said, I will go out as at other times, and shake myself free. And he did not know that the Lord had left him. And the Philistines seized him and gouged out his eyes…." (Judges 16:18-21).

This is the state of many in the Church: asleep in the lap of the world! Distracted and entertained by the things of the world, they miss what the Holy Spirit is saying and doing. They do not know the transforming power of the Holy Spirit. Samson reminds me of the many believers who never live out the plans and destinies that the Lord has specifically for them; believers who have a very limited vision of God's purposes and plans and give in to instant gratification and the pull of the world! Gifted and talented, they settle for the lusts of the flesh and live like people of the world. God's perspective, eternal rewards, fruitfulness are not in their thinking. They lack wisdom and discernment and don't understand that the enemy is a schemer with plans to destroy them. Peter says,

> "Be sober, be watchful. Your adversary the devil prowls around like a roaring lion, seeking some one to devour. (1 Peter 5:8).

It's interesting to note that the first thing the Philistines did to Samson was to take out his eyes! (Judges 16:21).

Ask yourself: Do you have a vision for your life? Do you know why you are alive in this planet? If you do, what are you doing about it? If you don't, you must ask the Lord to give you revelation of your destiny. How are you handling temptation and the pull of the world? Do you need deliverance from a spirit of sexual immorality? How are you using your eye gate? How are you engaging your imagination? What are you day dreaming about? Do you realize that the enemy has plans to destroy you? What kind of company do you keep? Are they helping you to walk with the Lord and fulfill your calling and destiny, or do they pull you away? What are you doing to keep the fire burning in your heart?

SAUL:
fear of man; pride; rebellion; jealousy.

Anointed to be the first king of Israel, Saul failed because of his pride, stubborness and disobedience to the Word of the Lord. He had fear of man and no fear of God! Proverbs 29:25 says,

"The fear of man lays a snare...."

Unable to trust and obey God, he was a "control freak" who allowed fear and circumstances to pressure him. In Samuel 13:8-14, he disobeyed the prophet Samuel and offered himself the burnt offering because "the people were scattering from me...." When David became a "threat" to him, Saul became insanely jealous and tried to kill David. He even built a monument for himself! (1 Samuel 12).

Saul is the type of leader who starts well and ends in disgrace; because of self-absorption and insecurity he could never really trust God. Roots of fear, jealousy and rebellion were never dealt with. He blamed others (just like Adam!) for his disobedience and never assumed responsibility for his actions. He was deceived and believed his own lies! We can say that he was full of HIMSELF! It's tragic when the Scriptures say twice that God was sorry that He had chosen Saul to be king:

> "The word of the Lord came to Samuel: I repent that I have made Saul king; for he has turned back from following me, and has not performed my commandments."
> (1 Samuel 15:10-11).

> "And the Lord repented that he had made Saul king over Israel." (1 Samuel 15:35b).

In 1 Samuel 15 the prophet Samuel gives Saul concrete orders of what to do with the Amalekites:

> "Now go and smite Amalek, and utterly destroy all that they have; do not spare them, but kill both man and woman, infant and suckling, ox and sheep, camel and ass." (1 Samuel 15:3).

Saul defeated the Amalekites, as commanded by the Lord, but only obeyed partially; he spared the king and the best of their flocks:

> "But Saul and the people spared Agag, and the best of the sheep and of the oxen and of the fatlings, and the lambs and all that was good, and would not utterly destroy them; all that was despised and worthless they utterly destroyed." (v.9).

What Saul saw and desired with his eyes was more important than obeying the Lord; he had no problem destroying "all that was despised and worthless," but spared "all that was good." Obedience is not obedience if it's only partial! He was so blinded to his disobedience that he told Samuel,"...I have performed the commandment of the Lord." (v.13). Then the excuse for his disobedience was this:

> "But the people took of the spoil, sheep and oxen, the best of the things devoted to destruction, to sacrifice to the Lord...." (v.21).

The prophet Samuel confronted Saul, but he blamed the people! Saul could not be corrected! He was blind to his disobedience and wrongdoing; therefore he could not assume responsibility for his actions.

Samuel's famous words are found in this chapter:

> "Has the Lord as great delight in burnt offerings
> and sacrifices,
> As in obeying the voice of the Lord?
> Behold, to obey is better than sacrifice,
> And to hearken than the fat of rams.
> For rebellion is as the sin of divination,
> And stubbornness is as iniquity and idolatry.
> Because you have rejected the word of the Lord,
> He has also rejected you from being king."
> (1 Samuel 15: 22-23).

It's not by accident that years later Saul's life ended by an Amalekite slaying him (2 Samuel 1:9-10). "Amalek" stands for our enemies: the flesh and the devil. Compromising with the enemy eventually leads to death; what you were supposed to "kill" and didn't "kill," will "kill" you! Beware! Paul says,

> "For the mind that is set on the flesh is hostile to God; it does not submit to God's law, indeed it cannot...." (Romans 8:7).

That was Saul's story: he was so set on the flesh that he could not submit to God. Throughout his reign Saul was "driven" by fear, insecurity and jealousy. At the end of his life he did what was forbidden: he went to consult a medium (1 Samuel 28:7); he turned to witchcraft in his desperation.

Ask yourself: Who's in control of your life? You or God? Are you led by the Spirit or are you in the flesh? How secure are you in the Father's love? Is there jealousy when you see others moving farther than you? Do you have a teachable spirit? How well do you receive correction? Do you accept responsibility for your actions, or do you blame others for your wrongdoings? How well are you obeying the Lord? Are you making compromises that cause you to disobey the Lord? How honest are you with the Lord and others? Is there love for the truth? Are your decisions based on faith or fear?

DAVID:
lust of the eyes; sexual immorality;

David's story aches my heart every time I read and think about it. But then I think of God's great mercy and grace and I'm blessed and encouraged! Today our Lord and Savior Jesus Christ seats on the "Throne of David"! God described David as "a man after my heart" (Acts 13:22). What caused such a great fall on one of God's greatest heroes of all times? Clearly the enemy used the eye gate to try to destroy King David. Let's take a look and try to understand so as not to make the same mistakes. Let's start with 2 Samuel 11:1-4:

> "In the spring of the year, the time when kings go forth to battle, David sent Joab, and his servants with him, and

> all Israel; and they ravaged the Ammonites, and besieged Rabbah. But David remained at Jerusalem. It happened, late one afternoon, when David arose from his couch and was walking upon the roof of the kings' house, that he saw from the roof a woman bathing; and the woman was very beautiful. And David sent and inquired about the woman. And one said, 'Is not this Bathsheba, the daughter of Eliam, the wife of Uriah the Hittite?' So David sent messengers, and took her; and she came to him, and he lay with her."

The first thing to notice is that David was in a place of disobedience. Being a king he was supposed to have gone out to battle in the spring, but he didn't. Instead he remained in Jerusalem. Right there we could say that there were cracks in God's protective shield over David's life. Why did David remain behind? Maybe he was tired of battling; tired of so many years of running away from Saul; tired of struggling. Now he had entered into his destiny, now the prophetic promised was fulfilled: he was king of Israel! He was enjoying victory and decided to take off his armor and relax. The thought of going back to war was not too attractive at that moment; he liked the comfort of the palace. He "felt" like taking it easy. Instead of asking the Lord to supply the grace to do the right thing, David remained behind and seriously slipped into great sin.

The Scriptures say that it was late in the afternoon when "David arose from his couch." It seems that David had been "lying around" most of the day, in contrast to his army who had gone to battle. Instead he walked on the roof of his house, and his "eyes" got him into trouble. Jesus says in Matthew 5:27-28,

> "You have heard that it was said, You shall not commit adultery. But I say to you that every one who looks at a woman lustfully has already committed adultery with her in his heart."

According to Jesus, using our eyes lustfully is equal to the sin of doing what we are lusting about!

In spite of the fact that Bathsheba was married to one of David's mighty men and also the daughter of Eliam (another of David's mighty men), David went ahead and asked for her! Clearly the lust of the eyes and the flesh took control at that moment; the temptation overpowered him. He not only committed adultery, but also betrayed his friends as he gave in to the lust of his eyes and flesh. One sin led to another sin as David eventually ordered Bathsheba's husband to be placed on the frontlines so that he would be killed by the enemy army.

Brothers and sisters, there are some important lessons to be learned from this passage of Scripture:

1. We need to stay in the place of obedience. In the place of obedience we remain abiding in Him with his protection covering us. The place of obedience is a solid foundation, while the place of disobedience is slippery.

   "He who dwells in the shelter of the Most High, who abides in the shadow of the Almighty,
   Will say to the Lord, My refuge and my fortress; my God in whom I trust.
   For He will deliver you from the snare of the fowler and from the deadly pestilence;
   He will cover you with his pinions and under his wings you will find refuge;
   His faithfulness is a shield and buckler. You will not fear the terror of the night,
   Nor the arrow that flies by day, nor the pestilence that stalks in darkness,
   Nor the destruction that wastes at noonday."
   (Psalm 91:1-6).

2. We need to rely on God's grace. No matter what is before us, or how weak we feel, we need to "see" that His grace is always available for us in order to overcome. As we stay in a place of humble dependence on the Lord, His grace will flow so that we can do His will at all times.

> "My grace is sufficient for you, for my power is made perfect in weakness." (2 Corinthians 12:9).

> "God opposes the proud but gives grace to the humble. Submit yourselves therefore to God. Resist the devil and he will flee from you." (James 4:6-7).

Humility is the door through which grace enters! Let's not depart from it!

3. We need to assume responsibility for our own personal battles instead of "lying on the couch," expecting others to fight our battles!

   I like Caleb's warrior spirit as he was taking his inheritance after forty years of walking in the wilderness:

> "I am still as strong to this day as I was in the day that Moses sent me; my strength now is as my strength was ten, for war, and for going and coming. So now give me this hill country...." (Joshua 14:11-12).

Ask yourself: Am I vigilant of the enemy's plans against my life and discerning of his subtle traps and snares? Am I in a place of submission to God so that I can resist the devil when he comes, or have my past victories given me a false sense of security? How am I availing myself of God's grace throughout the day, so that I run to Him immediately at the time of temptation? How am I using my eye gate? Am I using my eyes to focus on things above, or am I giving in to the lusts of the flesh by setting my mind on them? How am I responding when I experience great victories in my life?

SOLOMON:
lust of the eyes; sexual immorality; lack of vision; disobedience.

Who can understand what happened to Solomon? A king who started out so well, asking the Lord for wisdom, ended his reign doing the opposite of what God wanted! Quite frankly, he could not handle the riches and fame that came into his life! Could it also be that Solomon did not have a vision of his own, but only his father's vision?

> "At Gibeon the Lord appeared to Solomon in a dream by night; and God said, Ask what I shall give you....
> I am but a little child; I do not know how to go out or come in. And thy servant is in the midst of thy people whom thou hast chosen, a great people, that cannot be numbered or counted for multitude. Give thy servant therefore and understanding mind to govern thy people, that I may discern between good and evil; for who is able to govern this thy great people?" (1 Kings 3:5-9).

We see from this passage of Scripture that Solomon's heart was in the right place when he began to reign. He had a humble heart; he knew he needed God's wisdom to govern God's people, and he asked for "an understanding mind" instead of riches. God was so pleased with Solomon's request that He gave Solomon wisdom, plus riches and honor:

> "I give you also what you have not asked, both riches and honor, so that no other king shall compare with you...."
> (1 Kings 3:13).

1 Kings 4:29-31:

> "And God gave Solomon wisdom and understanding beyond measure, and largeness of mind like the sand on the seashore, so that Solomon's wisdom surpassed the wisdom of all the people of the east, and all the wisdom of Egypt. For he was wiser than all other men.and his fame was in all the nations round about."

1 Kings 11:23-25:

> "Thus King Solomon excelled all the kings of the earth in riches and in wisdom. And the whole earth sought the

> presence of Solomon to hear his wisdom, which God had put into his mind. Every one of them brought his present, articles of silver and gold, garments, myrrh, spices, horses, and mules, so much year by year."

However, the Lord had previously given the Israelites clear instructions of what their King should not do:

> "Only he must not multiply horses for himself, or cause the people to return to Egypt in order to multiply horses.... And he shall not multiply wives for himself, lest his heart turn away; nor shall he greatly multiply for himself silver and gold." (Deuteronomy 18:16-17).

> King Solomon did just the opposite! "All King Solomon's drinking vessels were of gold...Solomon gathered together chariots and horsemen...the king made silver as common in Jerusalem as stone...Solomon's import of horses was from Egypt and Kue." (1 Kings 10:21;26-28).

It's a sad commentary what 1 Kings 11:1-4 has to say about Solomon:

> "Now King Solomon loved many foreign women; the daughter of Pharaoh, and Moabite, Ammonite, Edomite, Sidonian, and Hittite women, from the nations concerning which the Lord has said to the people of Israel, 'You shall not enter into marriage with them, neither shall they with you, for surely they will turn away your heart after their gods.' Solomon clung to these in love. He had seven hundred wives, princesses, and three hundred concubines; and his wives turned away his heart. For when Solomon was old his wives turned away his heart after other gods...."

> What "gods" were this?

> "Ashtoreth the goddess of the Sidonians, Chemosh the

god of Moab, and Milcom the god of the Ammonites...." (1 Kings 11:33).

Ashtoreth: The Phoenician goddess of love and increase.
Chemosh: The powerful god of the Moabites that means to subdue.
Milcom: The national idol of the Ammonites that means to reign.

These, of course, were not "gods" but demonic forces at work in the heathen nations that captured Solomon's heart! Yes, the "goddess of love and increase" subdued him and reigned in his heart! I believe a powerful spirit of lust entered him through his eye gate. He couldn't have enough wives, gold, chariots and horses! Truly, Proverbs 27:20b was exemplified in his life:

"...never satisfied are the eyes of man."

The story of King Solomon is a sobering one! The Lord appeared to him twice and at the end of his life he was gripped by the enemy. You see, it's not only meeting Jesus, but persevering in the Spirit, staying in the race, learning how to flow in the rivers of grace so that we can overcome "the lust of the flesh and the lust of the eyes and the pride of life...." (1 John 2:16).

Ask yourself: Do I have my own personal vision from God for my life? Am I taking time on a daily basis to renew my mind with the Scriptures? How important is obedience to God's Word? Are God's blessings keeping me thankful and grateful to Him, knowing that He is my source, or have these blessings made me forget Him? How am I handling temptation? How am I justifying sin in my life?

RICH MAN:
(Parable of the Rich Man and Lazarus – Luke 16: 19-31): selfishness; avarice; lack of compassion.

The rich man in this parable stands for those who are indifferent and blind to the needs of others around them. They have no sensitivity, no compassion and no generosity for other people. This lack of compassion and hardness of heart stems from lack of relationship with the Lord and ignorance of His Word, due to pride and rebellion in their hearts. This kind of person is self-centered and ignores the poor and needy. When Sodom was destroyed, it was not only because of sexual sin, but also because of complacency and lack of compassion for the poor and needy:

> "Behold, this was the guilt of your sister Sodom: she and her daughters had pride, surfeit of food, and prosperous ease, but did not aid the poor and needy. They were haughty…." (Ezequiel 16: 49-50).

The rich man was blessed in every way; he was "clothed in purple and fine linen…..he feasted sumptuously every day." The Scriptures say that Lazarus, a poor man full of sores, was laid in the rich man's gate. In God's mercy, I believe that Lazarus was laid precisely at the rich man's gate for the benefit of the rich man! It was a God given opportunity for the rich man to show mercy and compassion. He failed miserably. In Acts 20:35, Paul says that we must help the weak and remember the words of the Lord Jesus,

> "It is more blessed to give than to receive."

As the rich man left and entered his home day in and day out, Lazarus was there at his gate; but he was blind to Lazarus. This man's heart had become calloused and insensitive. Lazarus had become "invisible" to the rich man! The rich man was too consumed with self to see Lazarus. When he finally "lifted up his eyes" (v.23) it was too late!

> "He who closes his ear to the cry of the poor will himself cry out and not be heard." (Proverbs 21:13).

Brothers and sisters, think of the "poor and needy" that God Himself has placed around you. Are you showing love and compassion towards them? Are you being generous with your time and finances?

"But if any one has the world's goods and sees his brother in need, yet closes his heart against him, how does God's love abide in him? Little children, let us not love in word or speech but in deed and in truth." (1 John 3:17-18).

Who are the "poor and needy" in your life? Are you reaching out to them or are you blind to their presence? Maybe it is your elderly neighbor, a widow, who has no help and a very limited income; maybe it is your friend who has been abandoned by her husband and is broken-hearted and broke! Maybe it's the single mother who is struggling to provide for her children! Open your eyes and see! Be led by the Holy Spirit and reach out and help the one(s) whom He is showing you!

"He who gives to the poor will not want, but he who hides his eyes will get many a curse." (Proverbs 28:27).

PHARISEE:
(Parable of the Pharisee and tax collector) (Luke 18:9-14): spirit of religiosity; legalism; judgmentalism.

The Pharisee in this parable stands for the kind of person who thinks he/she is better than everybody else and despises others who are not like him/her. Proverbs 30: 13 well describes them:

"There are those—how lofty are their eyes, how high their eyelids lift!"

Full of "self" and pride, they look down on others; they have a critical spirit and love to pass judgment. They only "look" at the negative in other people while blind to their own spiritual state; they focus on the form rather than the fruit. They are "self-righteous" (v9); they are legalistic and have no understanding of grace and no revelation of the Father's unconditional love. Jesus said in Matthew 23:24,

"Woe to you, scribes and Pharisees, hypocrites! For you cleanse the outside of the cup and of the plate, but inside

> they are full of extortion and rapacity. You blind Pharisee! First cleanse the inside of the cup and of the plate, that the outside also may be clean."

The Pharisees, being the most religious group at the time of Jesus, suffered from great spiritual blindness. I believe that there is a connection between a judgmental spirit and spiritual blindness. Jesus said,

> "Judge not, that you be not judged. For with the judgment you pronounce you will be judged, and the measure you give will be the measure you get. Why do you see the speck that is in your brother's eye, but do not notice the log that is in your own eye? Or how can you say to your brother, 'Let me take the speck out of your eye,' when there is the log in your own eye? You hypocrite, first take log out of your own eye, and then you will see clearly to take the speck out of your brother's eye." (Matthew 7:1-5).

I say "It's time to deal with the logs in our eyes!"
Proverbs 30:12 describes well the Pharisees:

> "There are those who are pure in their own eyes but are not cleansed of their filth."

Those "logs" of judgmentalism kept the Pharisees spiritually blind! They found fault with Jesus while at the same time clueless as to their terrible spiritual state. In Matthew 23, Jesus called them blind five times:

"blind guides" (v.16)
"blind fools" (v.17)
"blind men" (v.19)
"blind guides" (v.24)
"blind Pharisees" (v.26)

I think the Lord Jesus was trying to make a point! The Pharisees were blind spiritually even though they were spiritual leaders! How could they lead people to true knowledge of God when they themselves were blind spiritually?

> "Can a blind man lead a blind man? Will they not both fall into a pit?" (Luke 6:39).

These religious people looked good on the outside; they did all the "right things"; knew the Scriptures; but when the King of Glory came into their midst, they missed Him and killed Him because of their blindness! The Church is packed with people with this spirit still today! They are not open to the Holy Spirit and try to quench His power, doing the opposite of what the Lord desires. Romans 8: 8 says,

> "...those who are in the flesh cannot please God."

> Instead, we are to "walk by the Spirit" and "not gratify the desires of the flesh." (Galatians 5:16).

Ask yourself: How do I respond to people who are different than I? How do I respond to the "new" things of the Spirit? Am I critical and judgmental, or do I allow the Holy Spirit to lead me to truth and speak to me? Is my focus on the form rather than the fruit? Am I hearing the voice of God on a continual basis? Am I "majoring" on the minor things, rather on the things that are more important to the heart of God, such as seeing people getting saved, healed and delivered?

ANANIAS AND SAPPHIRA:
lying and deceit; dishonesty; hypocrisy.

> "Who shall ascend the hill of the Lord? And who shall
>   stand in his holy place?
> He who has clean hands and a pure heart, who does not
>   lift up his soul to what is false,
> And does not swear deceitfully." (Psalm 24: 3-4).

This couple could not "see" that lying was a serious thing! They wanted to impress others with their generosity and have them think that they were wonderful! They cared more about impressing people than impressing God! (Read Acts 4:32-37). Their "focus" was totally off!

> "...they loved the praise of men more than the praise of God." (John 12:43).

In Acts 5, Ananias comes to Peter pretending to give him all the proceeds from the sale of a property. Peter, with the gift of discernment of spirits, was able to "see" that Ananias was lying and told him:

> "Ananias, why has Satan filled your heart to lie to the Holy Spirit and to keep back part of the proceeds of the land.... How is it that you have contrived this deed in your heart? You have not lied to men but to God." (v.3-4).

The problem with Ananias was not that he kept part of the money; the problem was his dishonesty and lies. The Lord was so displeased with it, that He judged this sin immediately! Look at what happened to Ananias:

> "...he fell down and died" (v.5).

Three hours later his wife came to Peter and the same thing happened to her!

For many people today, lying has been "downgraded" to "acceptable." But not so with God! Jesus said,

> "Let what you say be simply Yes or No; anything more than this comes from evil." (Matthew 5:37).

Lying comes from the pit of hell! No matter the size or the "color" of the lie; it originates with the devil, who

> "...is a liar and the father of lies." (John 8:44).

As Christians, we are to resemble the Lord Jesus, Who is THE TRUTH incarnate! (John 14:6). Paul says,

> "Do not lie to one another, seeing that you have put off the old nature with its practices and have put on the new nature, which is being renewed in knowledge after the image of its creator." (Colossians 3:9-10).

Can't you "see" that lying is part of the old, sinful nature? As children of God we need to "put off the old nature" and "put on the new nature" in which lying does not belong.

Ask yourself: How do I view lying? Have I realized that "lying" comes from the enemy and it's one of his character traits? Do I minimize my lies, calling them "white lies?" How have I compromised with lies? Do I try to cover up my mistakes with lying? Do I fear what people think of me that I think I have to resort to lying?

Brothers and sisters, the above persons in this chapter started their race well but did not finish well, except for David. God loved them, He manifested Himself to them, they had an amazing destiny waiting for them, but most of the above never fulfilled completely what God had for them. Along the way they lost the vision! They got snared by sin, overpowered by temptation and gave in to the lusts of the flesh and eyes. Sin has a blinding effect on our lives so that we can't see clearly the truth about ourselves. Sin is an open door to the enemy where he can "legally" operate in our lives to destroy us. Like David, let's cry out to the Lord and tell Him:

> "Search me, O God, and know my heart! Try me and
> know my thoughts!
> And see if there be any wicked way in me….. "
> (Psalm 139:23-24).

I think it's time to get radical about tolerating and compromising with sin in our lives. I believe it's time to have every inner wound healed and leave no open doors in our spiritual houses to the enemy. I say it's time to forgive and not harbor resentment, bitterness, anger in our hearts. Let's keep a clean house where the Holy Spirit is loved and appreciated!

If you are harboring unforgiveness in your heart, it's time to avail yourself of the grace of God and in faith forgive every person that has harmed you in any way. Unforgiveness displeases God and makes you vulnerable to the enemy and blocks your spiritual vision. Unforgiveness is an open door for the enemy to destroy your life with sickness, disease, depression, fear, anxiety, confusion, darkness, etc. Matthew 18:23-35 clearly shows what happens to the person who does not forgive: he/she is handed over to the torturers!

Pray this (out loud):

"Heavenly Father, today I make a choice to forgive everyone who has hurt me in any way: those who have abused me in any way; those that have abandoned, rejected or neglected me in any way; those that have lied to me or lied about me; those who have stolen from me; those that have put me down again and again with their words and actions. I receive Your grace to forgive at this moment; I forgive these people (name them) and I release them into Your hands. I ask You, Lord, to bless them. I release all the anger, bitterness, resentment and hatred that I have carried in my heart. I not only forgive them but I also receive the grace to bless them. Create in me a clean and pure heart and fill me now with joy and gladness. Amen"

VII

LIGHT QUENCHERS!

Sin is a "light quencher!" Cursing father/mother, accepting bribes, perverting justice, greed, favoritism, alcoholism, hatred of others, are open doors through which darkness and spiritual blindness enter into our lives. These are some passages from the Scriptures worth meditating upon; ask the Holy Spirit to show you and give you revelation of your own "blind" spots so that you can repent and wash them away with the water of the Word:

> "If anyone curses his father of mother, his lamp will be put out in darkness." (Proverbs 20:20).
>
> "And you shall take no bribe, for a bribe blinds the officials, and subverts the cause of those who are in the right." (Exodus 23:).
>
> "You shall not pervert justice; you shall not show partiality; and you shall not take a bribe, for a bribe blinds the eyes of the wise and subverts the cause of the righteous." (Deuteronomy 16:19).
>
> "For the evil man has no future; the lamp of the wicked will be put out." (Proverbs 24:20).
>
> "Who has woe? Who has sorrow? Who has strife? Who has complaining? Who has wounds without cause? Who has redness of eyes? Those who tarry long over wine…

your eyes will see strange things, and your mind utter perverse things." (Proverbs 23: 29-33).

"Take heed lest there be a base thought in your heart, and you say, the seventh year, the year of release is near, and your eye be hostile to your poor brother, and you give him nothing, and he cry to the Lord against you, and it be sin in you." (Deuteronomy 15:9).

"Do not toil to acquire wealth; be wise enough to desist. When your eyes light upon it, it is gone; for suddenly it takes to itself wings…." (Proverbs 23:4-5)

"But he who hates his brother is in the darkness and walks in the darkness, and does not know where he is going, because the darkness has blinded his eyes." (1 John 2:11).

"My brethren, show no partiality as you hold the faith of our Lord Jesus Christ, the Lord of glory. For if a man with gold rings and in fine clothing comes into your assembly, and a poor man in shabby clothing also comes in, and you pay attention to the one who wears the fine clothing and say, 'Have a seat here, please,' while you say to the poor man, 'Stand there,' or, 'Sit at my feet,' have you not made distinctions among yourselves, and become judges with evil thoughts?" (James 2:1-4).

"Transgression speaks to the wicked deep in his heart; there is no fear of God before his eyes.
For he flatters himself in his own eyes that his iniquity cannot be found out and hated." (Psalm 36:1-2).

"The man of haughty looks and arrogant heart I will not endure." (Psalm 101:5b).

Another "light quencher" is the sin of occultism (Deuteronomy 18:9-14): Ouija-boards, horoscopes, palm reading, voodoo, Santeria, new age, channeling, spiritism, etc. This needs to be repented of and renounced! Involvement in the occult results in great darkness coming in through your eye-gate! It's time to repent and renounce it!

"Heavenly Father, I repent from my involvement in the occult. I renounce it and I ask You for forgiveness; cleanse me with Your precious blood. From now on I will turn to the Lord and to the Scriptures for guidance. I shut this door now on the enemy's face and in Jesus name command any evil spirits that came into my life to leave me now. Lord, fill me with your peace, joy and love for You and Your Word! Amen."

VIII

SUPERNATURAL VISION FOR THE MISSION!

"...for once you were darkness, but now you are light in the Lord; walk as children of light (for the fruit of light is found in all that is good and right and true), and try to learn what is pleasing to the Lord)" (Ephesians 5:8-10).

It's time to rise up and assume our place as children of the Most High! We are children of light and we are to release the light of Christ everywhere we go. We must "see" with His eyes and develop a kingdom mentality, seeking first His kingdom in every situation (Matthew 6:33). We are alive for such a time as this; the light shines brightest in deep darkness! The "marching orders" have been issued already:

"Go into all the world and preach the gospel to the whole creation.... And these signs will accompany those who believe: in my name they will cast out demons; they will speak in new tongues; they will pick up serpents, and if they drink any deadly thing, it will not hurt them; they will lay their hands on the sick, and they will recover." (Mark 16:15-18).

GET READY TO MOVE OUT OF YOUR COMFORT ZONE!

"Truly, truly, I say to you, he who believes in me will also do the works that I do; and greater works than these will he do, because I go to the Father." (John 14:12).

We are living in the time of the "greater works." Our minds need to be transformed and renewed with this truth. We need to see from God's perspective certain facts about ourselves. There is a purpose and plan for your life; you are not an accident or just one more number! Just like Jesus, you can say:

"The Spirit of the Lord is upon me, because he has
anointed me to preach good news to the poor.
He has sent me to proclaim release to the captives and
recovering of sight to the blind,
To set at liberty those oppressed…." (Luke 4:18).

For this purpose you have been gifted and there is no lack:

"…you are not lacking in any spiritual gift…."
(1 Corinthians 1:7).

Therefore, you are equipped to: PROCLAIM THE GOSPEL AND DEMONSTRATE ITS POWER!

"For the kingdom of God does not consist in talk but in power." (1 Corinthians 4:20).

For too long we have concentrated in giving nice talks! It's time to see the power of the gospel and to expect the Holy Spirit to confirm the Word being preached with miracles, signs and wonders! Look at what the Apostle Paul says:

"…and my speech and my message were not in plausible words of wisdom, but in demonstration of the Spirit and

> power, that your faith might not rest in the wisdom of men but in the power of God." (1 Corinthians 2:4-5).

The early Church prayed for a demonstration of the power of God:

> "...and grant to thy servants to speak thy word with all boldness, while thou stretchest out thy hand to heal, and signs and wonders are performed through the name of thy holy servant Jesus." (Acts 4:29-30).

Sirach 36:6 says,

> "Show signs anew, and work further wonders; make thy hand and thy right arm glorious."

Let's start using our eye gate and our imagination to engage in the great things the Lord wants to do in our midst today! Let's start "imagining" filling football stadiums to proclaim the gospel with a glorious demonstration of the power of God! Let's imagine thousands of people turning to Jesus in one night! How about great, miraculous healings, even creative miracles like missing legs and arms growing back! Yes, we need to start thinking big because we have a big God!

In Matthew 10:7-8, Jesus commanded his disciples to proclaim the kingdom of God and demonstrate its power. He said:

> "And preach as you go, saying, the kingdom of heaven is at hand. Heal the sick, raise the dead, cleanse lepers, cast out demons."

Therefore, the command is that "as you go" you must proclaim the gospel of the kingdom and demonstrate its power to heal the sick, raise the dead, cleanse lepers, cast out demons. Revelation of this truth must be received by every believer. This is normal Christian living; we are used to dysfunctional Christianity! So, "as you go" to work, to school, to the cleaners, to shop, be sensitive to the Holy Spirit, lift up your eyes to the Lord and let Him show you who you are supposed to minister to!

Say this: I CAN SHARE THE GOSPEL!

If you know Jesus personally and He is your Lord and Savior, you can tell people about him and give them an opportunity to repent and invite Jesus into their hearts. Don't worry about what words to use; just be a willing vessel and you will see how the Holy Spirit gives you the words you need to speak. Ask the Lord to place this desire in your heart!

> "...do not be anxious how you are to speak or what you are to say; for what you are to say will be given to you in that hour; for it is not you who speak, but the Spirit of your Father speaking through you." (Matthew 10: 19-20).

Say this: I CAN HEAL THE SICK!

We have been commissioned by the Lord to heal sick people. Jesus healed people everywhere He went and He wants His followers to do the same. The early Church obeyed His instructions and there was a great outpouring of Holy Spirit power; that's how the early Church grew! We have "gifts of healing" for this purpose (1 Corinthians 12:9). Today's Church must pick up that "mantle" of healing, just like Jesus!

Ask the Lord for opportunities to lay hands on the sick!

> "And they departed and went through the villages, preaching the gospel and healing everywhere." (Luke 9:6).

Say this: I CAN RAISE THE DEAD!

Yes, the Lord wants us to raise the dead, especially those who die young or die without knowing Jesus! We want to raise them back to life so that they have a chance to make a choice for Christ. The Lord wants everyone to be saved (1 Timothy 2:4). Jesus raised several dead people and in the book of Acts there are several examples of raising the dead.

Ask the Lord for this opportunity!

> "And he gave her his hand and lifted her up. Then calling the saints and widows he presented her alive.
> And it became known throughout all Joppa, and many believed in the Lord." (Acts 9:41-42).

Say this: I CAN CLEANSE LEPERS

In the name of Jesus we can cleanse people of physical, emotional or spiritual leprosy! Those infected, inner wounds need cleansing and healing so that we can keep advancing. They give the enemy a legal foothold in people's lives!

> "And he stretched out his hand and touched him, saying, I will; be clean. And immediately his leprosy was cleansed." (Matthew 8:3).

Say this: I CAN CAST OUT DEMONS!

Sure we can! According to Jesus, the first sign that accompanies believers is casting out demons! (Mark 16:15-17). The enemy has already been defeated by the Blood of Jesus; all we need to do is exercise our authority in Jesus' name and cast those spirits out.

> "...But Paul was annoyed, and turned and said to the spirit, I charge you in the name of Jesus Christ to come out of her. And it came out that very hour." (Acts 16:18).

LORD, I NEED VISION FOR MY TONGUE!

> "Death and life are in the power of the tongue, and those who love it will eat its fruits." (Proverbs 18:21).

Our fallen tongue is a big problem! (James 3:1-12). The way we use our tongue will ultimately determine our victory or our defeat. You must "see" this! Our words are power-packed for good or evil! In the world I picked up many negative and ungodly ways of using my tongue, like criticizing, gossiping, grumbling and complaining, which are detestable in the eyes of God and produce death. I had to give it up and start speaking in a different way that produced life. As the people of God we need to grow up and learn the ways of the Spirit; one of the basic truths we need to learn is that our tongue releases either "death" or "life." We need to assume personal responsibility for the correct use of our tongue and not use it irresponsibly to grumble, complain, criticize, gossip, accuse, slander, lie; this grieves the Holy Spirit:

> "Let no evil talk come out of your mouths, but only such as is good for edifying, as fits the occasion, that it may impart grace to those who hear. And do not grieve the Holy Spirit of God, in whom you were sealed for the day of redemption. Let all bitterness and wrath and anger and clamor and slander be put away from you…."
> (Ephesians 4:29-31).

Our nasty words not only grieve the Holy Spirit, but they make us stumble:

> "…he who opens wide his lips comes to ruin."
> (Proverbs 13:3b).

> "O that a guard were set over my mouth, and a seal of prudence upon my lips, that it may keep me from falling, so that my tongue may not destroy me!" (Sirach 22:27).

Yes, our words can keep the Holy Spirit grieved and quenched at the time when we need Him the most, and our tongue can ruin our lives. Instead, we need to rise up in faith and use our tongue to release life and God's plans and purposes, in spite of what we see with our natural eyes. This is called FAITH!

We are called to be "light" in this generation; our grumbling and wrong use of our tongue can actually block the light of Jesus from shining through us:

> "Do all things without grumbling or questioning, that you may be blameless and innocent, children of God without blemish in the midst of a crooked and perverse generation, among whom you shine as lights in the world…." (Philippians 2:14-15).

My friend, who owns a clothing store, was not doing great during this "bad" economy in the Christmas season. Someone prophesied to her that a financial breakthrough was coming.

From that moment on she just praised and thanked the Lord, and then her breakthrough came! In less than one week just one person came into the store and spent $6000! She gives glory to the Lord and has seen the power of the prophetic word!

Our true reality is not what we see with our natural eyes, so this is why we need the Holy Spirit to show us what we need to know so that we can release His plans and strategies. Jeremiah 33:33:

> "Call to me and I will answer you, and will tell you great and hidden things which you have not known."

What the Lord shows and tells us, this is what we believe and on that revelation we stand. This is what we decree and declare with our mouths. In the meantime, we thank and praise the Lord and flow in the spirit, moving mountains, proclaiming the Word of God, calling the things that are not as though they were, blessing God and others.

What are some of the ways in which we should use our tongues?

THANK GOD!

> "...always and for everything giving thanks in the name of our Lord Jesus Christ to God the Father."
> (Ephesians 5:20).

Instead of blaming others and pointing the finger at them, start thanking the Lord by faith for the breakthrough. Stop looking at people and start looking at Jesus; become a doer of God's word, which says,

> "...give thanks in all circumstances; for this is the will of God in Christ Jesus for you. Do not quench the Spirit."
> (1 Thessalonians 5:18-19).

Even if you don't understand what is going on, start thanking the Lord in the midst of what you're going through. This is His will for you at that moment: to THANK HIM! This means opening your mouth and releasing thanksgiving out loud. Thanking God is the first step into His presence:

> "Enter his gates with thanksgiving, and his courts with praise!" (Psalm 100:4).

Thanking the Lord releases great power in the Spirit realm; miracles (John 6:11); breakthroughs (2 Chronicles 20:21); healings (Luke 17:15-19); deliverances (Jonah 2:9-10); are released. We must learn to thank Him at all times; in the good, the bad and the ugly! Usually what happens when we face difficulties and setbacks is that we use our tongue in the wrong way, thereby quenching the Spirit when we most need Him!

> "Let there be no filthiness, nor silly talk, nor levity, which are not fitting; but instead let there be thanksgiving." (Ephesians 5:4).

My friend needed to sell at least one house in order to pay her bills; she had experienced a great financial setback and had no cash flow. I told her to come to my house; my prayer partner was with me and we were praising the Lord. When my friend arrived we just thanked the Lord for being so good and faithful; we thanked Abba for being a good father. As we continued thanking the Lord, her cell phone rang with the news that one house had sold! On her way back home she received another phone call that another house had sold! Thank You, Jesus! Paul says,

> "Rejoice in the Lord always; again I will say, rejoice. Let all men know your forbearance. The Lord is at hand. Have no anxiety about anything, but in everything by prayer and supplication with thanksgiving let your requests be made known to God. And the peace of God, which passes all understanding, will keep your hearts and your minds in Christ Jesus." (Philippians 4:6-7).

First of all, it's your choice to rejoice! No matter what you are going through, you can choose to rejoice in the Lord because He is so wonderful and He is our reality. Make Jesus and His kingdom your reality; David says,

> "I keep the Lord always before me; because he is at my right hand, I shall not be moved." (Psalm 16:8).

What do you keep always before you? What are you looking at with the eyes of your heart? (If all you think about is the problem and the difficulty, you are using your eye gate in the wrong way and more darkness will come in.)

Then, as we pray with thanksgiving, the peace of God will guard our hearts and minds from "the flaming darts " (Ephesians 6:16) of lies and doubts from the enemy. Rejoicing in the Lord will help you stay in thanksgiving which will help you stay in the peace of God and focused on Him and His promises.

Rejoicing + Thanksgiving = Peace!

> "I will praise the name of God with a song; I will
> magnify him with thanksgiving.
> This will please the Lord more than an ox or a bull with
> horns and hoofs." (Psalm 69:30-31).

PRAISE AND WORSHIP HIM!

> "Let everything that breathes praise the Lord!"
> (Psalm 150:6).

Learn to praise your way through your difficulties; you must "see" this! Substitute your grumbling and complaining with praises to our God! Learn to praise and give glory to God with all of your being as you go through trials and tribulation. Create an atmosphere, especially at that moment of difficulty, where the Holy Spirit can thrive and be Himself. Most people are very passive about praising the Lord; they think they have to "feel like it" in order to do it, or that it's just an option. Others think that praising the Lord has to do with personality type! If the Lord says hundreds of times in the Scriptures to praise Him, I think that He means it!

Especially during difficulties, we must rise up in faith and start to praise Him; we will be changed in His presence as we build Him a "throne." He will fight our battles in that kind of atmosphere. Remember there is power in your tongue! Our words are packed with power for life or death (Proverbs 18:21) in the spirit realm, which will cause changes in the natural realm. As you go through the valley of weeping, your praises will cause your desert to be changed into a "place of springs" and you will go "from strength to strength"(Psalm 84:6). Through it all the Lord is building His character in you and strengthening your faith muscles, because "...without faith it is impossible to please him." (Hebrews 11:6).

The Lord is worthy to be praised! He inhabits our praises (Psalm 22:3); our praises create a "platform" for Him to come and extend His kingdom in our lives and situations. Psalm 87: 2 says,

> "...the Lord loves the gates of Zion more than all the dwelling places of Jacob."

What are the gates of Zion? The gates of praise! Where are those gates located? In your mouth!

We cannot allow our circumstances to control us; we cannot allow our flesh to control us; we cannot allow our five senses to control us; we cannot allow the enemy to control us with his lies and deceptions! In the difficulty, in the stress, in the trial, we overcome by rising up to give praise to our King because He is worthy to be praised! We change the atmosphere with the high praises!

> "Through Him then let us continually offer up a sacrifice of praise to God, that is, the fruit of lips that acknowledge his name." (Hebrews 13:15).

It is there, in the place of praise, that He fights your battles! Remember that we are not fighting flesh and blood, but invisible enemies that have been released against us to keep us from advancing.

Praise releases His presence and in His presence we find:

The atmosphere of heaven
(Revelation 4:8; 5:9-10; 11:17-18; 15:3-4;)

Victory over the enemy because praise is a weapon of warfare
(Psalm 149; 2 Chronicles 20:21-23; Isaiah: 42:10-13).

Freedom (2 Corinthians 3:17).

Transformation (2 Corinthians 3:18).

Deliverance (Acts 16:25-26).

Fullness of joy (Psalm 16:11).

Revelation (Ephesians 1:17).

Angelic ministry (Psalm 103:20).

Healing (Psalm 147:1-3).

Miracles (Psalm 146).

A wonderful "side effect" of praising the Lord is that in His presence we forget about ourselves; we go from being self-conscious to becoming God-conscious as we focus on His greatness! That in itself is a big healing! Remember that it was in the garden through disobedience that Adam and Eve became self-conscious and realized they were naked! Our self-image is dealt with as we praise the Lord, because His presence is released through the "high" praises (halals and tehillahs) that makes us look like fools, just like David in 1 Samuel 6! The fear of man that keeps us paralyzed and neutralized is broken in this kind of atmosphere so that we are freed, not only to praise and worship Him in the way He asks, but to serve Him in the power of the Spirit!

PROPHESY!

> "...he who prophesies speaks to men for their upbuilding, and encouragement and consolation."
> (1 Corinthians 14:3).

Quit the hopelessness and start listening to God's voice so that you can prophesy into that situation. We need His perspective. God has a plan, a strategy, a solution for that situation; whatever you are going through has not taken Him by surprise! He is not worried.

All of us can prophesy (1 Corinthians 14:31)! What does it mean to prophesy? It means to hear from God, believe it and speak it. Jesus said in John 10:27,

> "My sheep hear My voice...."

Are you His sheep? Then you can hear His voice! On the day of Pentecost, Peter quoted the prophet Joel:

> "And in the last days it shall be, God declares, that I will
> pour out my Spirit upon all flesh,
> And your sons and your daughters shall prophesy...."
> (Acts 2:17).

Are you His son or daughter? Then you can prophesy!

What's so important about the prophetic word? Why is it so important to speak it out?

The prophetic word comes from the heart of God; it's the Lord speaking through a human vessel. It is God's report, plan, strategy for that person, for that difficulty, for that family, for that business, for that nation, etc. It is a word from the throne of God; therefore, when it is released it is power-packed because the Lord

> "confirms the word of his servant, and performs the counsel of his messengers...." (Isaiah 44:26).

The Lord told the prophet Jeremiah,

"I am watching over my word to perform it."
(Jeremiah 1:12).

The Lord is totally committed to His Word spoken through His servants. He says that He will "confirm" and "perform" it! The prophetic word causes a shift in the spiritual realm which will cause changes in the natural. That's why prophets exist and that's why we are prophetic: so that the Lord can release His voice, His plans, His thoughts through His people and cause changes to occur in the natural according to His perfect will. We are called to live a supernatural life in this planet; how can we do this if we are blind and deaf spiritually?

Praying in tongues and praising the Lord with the high praises will break open your wells. We have "wells of salvation" (Isaiah 12:3) and when they break open, the rivers of living water (John 7:38) will start flowing, and there is the voice of the Lord! Psalm 29:3 says,

"The voice of the Lord is upon the waters...."

Last year in Yumbe, Uganda, the Lord gave me a word of knowledge (revelation from the Lord) that there were people in the meeting who needed cars. Suddenly I remembered that Fr. Stephen was hoping for a car; I turned to him and prophesied to him that a car was coming. Another word of knowledge came that the Lord was healing teeth and gums and many people raised their hands in faith to receive that specific healing. Last month (a year later) we went back to Yumbe, and it was a joy to have Fr. Stephen pick us up at the airport with his new vehicle! Not only that, he showed us a complete healing of a loose tooth that was healed after that word of knowledge! Isn't God good?

2 Chronicles 20:20 says,

"Believe in the Lord your God, and you will be established; believe his prophets, and you will succeed."

DECREE AND DECLARE

"Thou shalt decree a thing, and it shall come to thee, and light shall shine in thy ways." (Job 22:28)
(The Holy Bible-Douay Version).

The Word of God says that when we "decree a thing" it shall come to pass! This is the power and authority that the Lord has given us in our tongue, so that His kingdom can be extended on earth! Do you "see" it? This is why we need to look into the Spirit realm and decree and declare what the Lord shows us, not what we see with our natural eyes. We need to get into the habit of making bold decrees and declarations from the Word of God and prophetic revelation the Lord gives us, thereby releasing life, healing, light, restoration, into the nations, into people's lives and circumstances. We decree and declare both what the Holy Spirit shows us and what the Scriptures say.

We decree and declare the solution, the breakthrough, the victory, the healing, the restoration, the abundance, the joy, the peace, the love, etc. Papa loves us and has good plans for us! There is no lack in the Kingdom!

Last month in Pallisa, Uganda, we were ministering in a church without windows. Yes, no windows! And no air conditioning! It was very hot, the church was very crowded and there was too much sweat! I took authority over the temperature in the name of Jesus and "decreed and declared" a drop in temperature. Within a few hours, the temperature dropped to such an extent that I had to wear a shawl!

I have been decreeing and declaring the blessings of God found in Deuteronomy 28:1-14 over my family and the people that I pray for on a continual basis. I have seen a release of the favor of God upon them; even my two daughters-in-laws are signs of God's favor! Proverbs 18:22 says,

"He who finds a wife finds a good thing, and obtains favor from the Lord."

Fathers, mothers, grandparents, cultivate a habit of decreeing and declaring the blessings of Almighty God over the children. As you do so, you create "an atmosphere" of blessing around them; light is released as you do so (Job 22:28) and you will see those words come to pass!

MOVE MOUNTAINS!

Instead of talking about your mountains all day long, start speaking to them and commanding them out of your life! Jesus said it!

> "Truly, I say to you, whoever says to this mountain, be taken up and cast into the sea, and does not doubt in his heart, but believes that what he says will come to pass, it will be done for him." (Mark 11:23).

We are a mountain-moving people; we not only remove those obstacles, but we replace them with the blessing. We leave no vacuum in the spirit realm! Mountains of division, strife, contentions in our families, prayer groups, jobs, are replaced with the fruit of the Holy Spirit: love, joy, peace (Galatians 5:22); mountains of financial insufficiency are replaced with God's provision (Philippians 4:19), which is always more than enough! Mountains of depression and sadness are replaced with the joy of the Lord, which is our strength! (Nehemiah 8:10). Mountains of sickness and disease are replaced with the healing of the Kingdom, because "by His wounds we have been healed" (1 Peter 2:24).

I like the passage in Zechariah 4 about the mountain. The Lord said,

> "What are you, O great mountain? Before Zerubbabel you shall become a plain; and he shall bring forward the top stone amid shouts of Grace, grace to it!"

We need to "see" all the mountains in our lives become a plain! He has given us the power to remove them!

Going to the nations can be very expensive, especially when

one goes to third world countries where you have to pay your own way most of the time. I know that when the Lord calls He provides, but it is up to us to remove the mountains that block the provision. Sometimes there are even curses of poverty, for example, coming down the family tree that is giving the enemy a legal right to "sit" on that mountain and block God's provision. We need to discern the mountains in our lives and become spiritual "bulldozers" and see each mountain become a plain!

The Lord says in Isaiah 41:15-16,

> "Behold, I will make of you a threshing sledge, new,
> sharp, and having teeth;
> You shall thresh the mountains and crush them, and you
> shall make the hills like chaff;
> You shall winnow them and the wind shall carry them
> away, and the tempest shall scatter them.
> And you shall rejoice in the Lord; in the Holy One of
> Israel, you shall glory."

One of the biggest mountains we have is the mountain of unbelief. Unbelief will hinder you from entering into your promised land and living the abundant life that Jesus came to bring (John 10:10). Through the difficult times the Lord is trying to teach us to walk by faith and not by sight, because "...without faith it is impossible to please Him" (Hebrews 11:6). This includes seeing into the invisible realm, hearing His voice, using our tongue for life and not death!

Psalm 97:3 says that "The mountains melt like wax before the Lord...." Praise and worship Him and see those mountains melt in His glorious presence!

CALL THE THINGS THAT ARE NOT AS THOUGH THEY WERE!

> "...who gives life to the dead and calls into existence the things that do not exist." (Romans 4:17).

Stop the negative thinking and constant repetition of all the problems, and instead start using your mouths to release God's will into that situation. Jesus taught us how to pray to the Father, asking Him for His kingdom and His will to come "on earth as it is in heaven." Start calling those things on earth that are not like heaven as though they were!

This is how God operates; doesn't make sense to the natural mind, but we are called to live in the supernatural realm, seeing the end from the beginning and speaking it out.

> "...or I am God, and there is no other; for I am God, and there is none like me, declaring the end from the beginning and from ancient times things not yet done, saying, My counsel shall stand, and I will accomplish all my purpose...." (Isaiah 46:9-10).

Look at the power the Lord gives to names:

God changed Abram's name to Abraham, meaning "father of many nations," when Isaac was not even born!

Jesus changed Simon's name to Peter, meaning "rock," when he was anything but a rock!

The Lord called Gideon "mighty man of valor" when he was hiding because of fear!

Every time the new name was spoken, it released power in the Spirit realm to fulfill its meaning!

Father Abraham learned to live in this realm of faith as he waited for the promise of God to be fulfilled. Over twenty-five years Abraham waited for the birth of Isaac, the child of the promise:

> "In hope he believed against hope, that he should become the father of many nations; as he had been told, so shall your descendants be. He did not weaken in faith when he considered his own body, which was as good as dead because he was about a hundred years old, or when he

> considered the barrenness of Sarah's womb. No distrust made him waver concerning the promise of God, but he grew strong in his faith as he gave glory to God, fully convinced that God was able to do what he had promised." (Romans 4:18-21).

Are you fully convinced that the Lord is able to do what He has promised you?

PROCLAIM THE WORD OF GOD!

Instead of proclaiming people's opinions, start releasing "swords" out of your mouth! The Word of God becomes "the sword of the Spirit" (Ephesians 6:17) when quickened by the Holy Spirit. It is a powerful sword that defeats the enemy, because the devil is a liar and the word of God is truth.

> Tell the Lord: "Make my mouth like a sharp sword…." (Isaiah 49:2).

The strongholds in our minds (2 Corinthians 10:4-5) where we have been believing lies from the enemy will come tumbling down as the hammer of the Word of God (Jeremiah 23:29) shatters them and as the light of the Word of God (Psalm 119:130) penetrates to dispel the darkness out of our mindsets.

I remember when I faced an "impossible" court case and all the "experts" said it was impossible for me to win. I started to research the Scriptures to find the heart of God concerning justice, and I found that the Lord is a lover of justice and that He wants justice in the courts. I wrote down every Scripture passage that I found that dealt with the difficulty I was facing and I started to proclaim those Scriptures with authority. In the Spirit I felt that the Word of God was being released like bombs in the enemy camp! My mind was renewed to believe the Lord for victory! His love for me, his love for justice, His faithfulness, became such a reality that I knew that victory was mine! And it was!

One Scripture verse regarding justice, that has stayed stuck in my mind and heart is this:

> "For the Lord loves justice; he will not forsake his saints."
> (Psalm 37:28).

The Holy Spirit quickens passages from the Bible to speak to us personally. Those passages become a sword that comes out of our mouths as we speak them out.

In one of my ministries in Tanzania, there was a "good" Catholic man that attended the seminar for a few days. I made an invitation for those people that were not baptized in the Spirit nor spoke in tongues to come to the front and receive this blessing. This man literally ran to the front to receive the Holy Spirit. He was "hungry" for more! We laid hands on him and the Spirit came in power. Afterwards, the Holy Spirit prompted this proverb:

> "Do you see a man skillful in his work? He will stand
> before kings;
> He will not stand before obscure men." (Proverbs 22:29).

We had a sense that there was something "big" that God had planned for this man. That "sword" was spoken over his life; after that he went to a job interview. Since then he has become the rector of a major university and the Lord is using him powerfully there to extend His kingdom, opening prayer groups on campus and making it possible for the students to pray and grow in the Spirit! This is only the beginning!

> "For as the rain and the snow come down from heaven,
> and return no thither but water the earth,
> Making it bring forth and sprout, giving seed to the
> sower and bread to the eater,
> So shall my word be that goes forth from my mouth; it
> shall not return to me empty,
> But it shall accomplish that which I purpose, and prosper
> in the thing for which I sent it." (Isaiah 55:10-11).

PRAY/INTERCEDE!

"Ask, and it will be given you; seek, and you will find;
knock and it will be opened to you.
For every one who asks receives, and he who seeks finds,
and to him who knocks it will be opened.
Or what man of you, if his son asks him for bread, will
give him a stone?
Or if he asks for a fish, will give him a serpent?
If you then, who are evil, know how to give good gifts to
your children, how much more will your Father who is in
heaven give good things to those who ask him!"
(Matthew 7:7-11).

Substitute your criticism with prayer and intercession! Papa wants to "give us good things." Make use of your priestly anointing to go before the throne of mercy and grace:

"Let us then with confidence draw near to the throne of grace, that we may receive mercy and find grace to help in time of need." (Hebrews 4:16).

Sometimes we forget there is such a place!

If you are so desperate that you cannot pray, thank or praise the Lord, start praying in tongues! This is a great weapon and it will break open your wells of salvation, thereby releasing the "rivers of living water" (John 7:38), and your inner man will be strengthened (1 Corinthians 14:4).

Paul says,

"Likewise the Spirit helps us in our weakness; for we do not know how to pray as we ought, but the Spirit himself intercedes for us with sighs too deep for words."
(Romans 8:26).

Our wonderful helper, the Holy Spirit, is there to help us in our weakness! It's actually good to reach this point, where we see our own weakness, where we know that we can't do it on our own! "Not by might, nor by power, but by my Spirit, says the Lord of hosts" (Zechariah 4:6). It's in that place of weakness that our eyes are lifted up to the Lord, knowing that only He can help. Humbling ourselves before the Lord is a good thing, because

> "God opposes the proud, but gives grace to the humble." (James 4:6).

The Lord told Paul in 2 Corinthians 12:9:

> "My grace is sufficient for you, for my power is made perfect in weakness."

Paul was able to say then:

> "I will all the more gladly boast of my weaknesses, that the power of Christ may rest upon me. For the sake of Christ, then, I am content with weaknesses, insults, hardships, persecutions, and calamities; for when I am weak, then I am strong." (2 Corinthians 12:10).

We have to learn from the Apostle Paul and appropriate this truth: it's in a place of weakness that the power of Christ will rest upon us! Do you "see" it? Experiencing weakness is not an excuse not to pray, because in that weakness the Holy Spirit will be released powerfully. Paul was not afraid of experiencing trials and difficulties that caused him to come face to face with his own weakness and inability to cope; he had learned that in his weakness, then he was strong because the power of Christ would flow through him mightily.

Last month in Uganda, on our outreach to the pygmies, we encountered a pygmy who was hiding behind the bushes so that we wouldn't see him. When he finally came out, I "saw" rejection, abandonment, shame, pain, all over him. He was pretty small and his nickname was "Small Dog." Quite frankly, at that moment I didn't even know how to pray for him or what to pray for. My heart was bursting with compassion; all I could do was place my hand over his heart and say from the depths of my heart "Jesus, please love this man." I prayed in the Spirit and we saw this man's countenance changed. The Holy Spirit released the love of Jesus into his heart and joy came upon him. In my weakness, the Lord did a mighty work, and the glory goes to Him!

All of us have an assigned place in the "spiritual" walls around our "land" where we are supposed to watch, pray and intercede. As we spend time with the Lord, He will show us things to come to prepare us so that our families, churches, nations can be protected from the attacks of the enemy. For example, I know that many people have been praying that the plans of terrorists for destruction be exposed before they cause harm. Have you seen how many terrorists have been captured before their plans take place? This is the result of intercession! When we intercede, the Holy Spirit intervenes!

> "Upon your walls, O Jerusalem, I have set watchmen;
> All the day and all the night they shall never be silent.
> You who put the Lord in remembrance, take no rest,
> And give him no rest until he establishes Jerusalem
> And makes it a praise in the earth." (Isaiah 62:6-7).

BLESS

> "The wise man makes himself beloved through his words...." (Sirach 20:13).

Cultivate the habit of blessing the Lord and blessing people everywhere you go. You become a blessing in the process!

I was ministering in Texas close to the Mexican border. I was taken to a wonderful Mexican restaurant; as soon as I saw the waiter, I knew the Lord wanted me to reach out to him. I asked the Lord for revelation about this man. As the waiter left and went to get lemonade, the Lord showed me that this man wanted wisdom and had been searching for it in the wrong places. When he came back, boldly I told him that I saw that he was a seeker of wisdom, but that he had been searching in many different places without finding it. I said to him, "You don't need to go searching and searching, when Jesus is the Wisdom of God (Colossians 2:3)! In Jesus you will find all the wisdom that you need, and he freely offers it to you!" He looked at me and said, "Are you a psychic?" He was shaken! I identified myself as a Catholic Charismatic and explained to him that I was just using the gifts of the Holy Spirit. I was able to share the gospel with this waiter and told him that he needed to make a decision for Christ if he wanted forgiveness and a new life. He was a fallen away Catholic. We left. The following day I was asked "Where do you want to go for lunch?" Immediately I said, "The Mexican restaurant!"

We went back to the Mexican restaurant, and the moment our waiter saw us, he ran towards us, bringing another waiter and saying "You must speak to this one; he needs it!" Our waiter shared with us that when he got home the previous day he opened his heart to Jesus and invited Him as his Lord and Savior. Alleluia! This man's countenance had even changed!

Become a blessing to others by giving them a prophetic word or word of knowledge about their destiny when they are going through tough times. Instead of talking and talking about a loved one's problems and difficulties, instead get into the Spirit realm and ask the Lord for revelation for that person. That word will lift them up and encourage them tremendously.

> "Anxiety in a man's heart weighs him down, but a good word makes him glad." (Proverbs 12:25).

> "Pleasant words are like a honeycomb, sweetness to the soul and health to the body." (Proverbs 16:24).

We need this truth constantly before our eyes:

The Lord has amazing plans for every person! We need to keep this truth in front of us always, so that we don't settle for what we see with our natural eyes:

> "What no eye has seen, nor ear heard, nor the heart of man conceived, what God has prepared for those who love him." (1 Corinthians 2:9).

I don't care what the person looks like or what the situation is; that is not the final word from the throne! What you see is not the final chapter in their lives! We have "rivers of living water" flowing from deep within that releases supernatural revelation (words of knowledge, wisdom, prophecy) so that we can speak what the Lord shows us and release blessings as we go.

> "...the fountain of wisdom is a gushing stream."
> (Proverbs 18:4b).

Even our "enemies" we should be blessing, thereby overcoming evil with good. Jesus says to

> "...bless those who curse you...." (Luke 7:28).

Peter says,

> "Do not return evil for evil or reviling for reviling; but on the contrary bless, for to this you have been called, that you may obtain a blessing." (1Peter 3:9).

LORD, I NEED VISION FOR THE USE OF MY TIME!

> "Look carefully then how you walk, not as unwise men but as wise, making the most of the time, because the days are evil." (Ephesians 5:15).

We need to "see" time as a God-given gift. James says that we are a

> "mist that appears for a little time and then vanishes."
> (James 4:14).

The time we spend on earth is like a vapor, compared to eternity! We are on this planet for a very short time, so let's try to make it as fruitful as possible for the sake of King Jesus!

David says in Psalm 39:4-5,

> "Lord, let me know my end, and what is the measure of my days;
> Let me know how fleeting my life is!
> Behold, thou hast made my days a few handbreadths,
> And my lifetime is as nothing in thy sight.
> Surely every man stands as a mere breath!"

Jesus changes our perspective when He says,

> "Do not lay up for yourselves treasures on earth, where moth and rust consume and where thieves break in and steal, but lay up for yourselves treasures in heaven, where neither moth nor rust consumes and where thieves do not break in and steal." (Matthew 6:19-20).

The Lord challenges us to look at our focus and perspective in this life. Are we living here gripped with an earthly perspective, with the focus of establishing and expanding our own kingdom, not realizing that "earthly" things will pass away and not endure? Or am I living for Him, expanding His kingdom and storing treasure in heaven, which will last forever? There is nothing wrong with making money and being wealthy; these are blessings from God. But if this becomes our goal we are falling into the danger of money becoming an idol! Jesus says,

> "But first seek his kingdom and his righteousness, and all these things shall be yours as well." (Matthew 6:33).

When Matthew 6:33 becomes our perspective, our whole outlook in life will change; we will start bearing fruit and storing treasure in heaven as we put God's kingdom first. We will have a kingdom mentality and will release the kingdom everywhere we go. The Lord will give us a heart for people and a holy boldness to release His love and power. Our desire should be to give Jesus the reward of His sufferings: human beings. He actually loves the human race!

We in North America have been blessed with "time." We have so much free time as compared to people in third world countries! For example, we have washers, dryers, dishwashers, running water, electricity, pampers, cars. All these conveniences make life much easier and less time consuming. I say this because as God's people we have a responsibility to use our time wisely. What will bear more fruit, watching television or interceding for the nation? Gossiping on the telephone or witnessing on the streets? Playing bingo or mentoring a young believer?

There is a reason, a plan, a purpose why you are alive at this time in the history of the human race. You do not want to miss it! There is a divine destiny for you down here, where you bear fruit in abundance for the glory of God! Give the Lord your time and ask Him to put your day in His divine order. Give Him your schedule and allow Him to show you how to use your time, so that you can be a fruitful citizen of His Kingdom. Ask Him to turn your affections toward what He thinks is important; ask Him to give you the desire to love the things that He loves and to hate the things that He hates!

LORD, I NEED VISION FOR MY FINANCES!

> "If then you have not been faithful in the unrighteous mammon, who will entrust to you the true riches?" (Luke 16:11).

According to Jesus, before we can be trusted with "the true riches" we need to be found faithful in the way we handle our finances. So what are the "true riches?" I believe the "true riches" include many things: revelation, intimacy with the Lord, the anointing, a ministry, God's people, shalom, authority, favor, etc.

It's very clear in the Scriptures, that as God's people we are to tithe and give our offerings on a continuous basis. This started with Abraham, the father of our faith. Tithing and giving offerings causes us to trust the Lord as our source. It's also one of the highest forms of worship! But something wonderful happens when we give our tithes and offerings: as we obey, we position ourselves in a place to be blessed by the Lord! Since the moment I began to tithe and give offerings, there has been great joy in my heart and I have not lacked anything. Look at this verse from Proverbs 3:9-10:

> "Honor the Lord with your substance and with the first
> fruits of all your produce;
> Then your barns will be filled with plenty, and your vats
> will be bursting with wine."

No matter if the world's economy is being shaken, in the "kingdom" there are no economic problems! We have received "a kingdom that cannot be shaken" (Hebrews 12:28). Imagine what it is to live without fear, worry, and anxiety about your life!

Malachi 3:10-12 states clearly the blessings that are released on our lives when we tithe and give offerings:

> "Bring the full tithes into the storehouse, that there may be food in my house; and thereby put me to the test, says the Lord of hosts, if I will not open the windows of heaven for you and pour down for you and overflowing blessing. I will rebuke the devourer for you, so that it will not destroy the fruits of your soil; and your vine in the field shall not fail to bear, says the Lord of hosts. Than all nations will call you blessed, for you will be a land of delight, says the Lord of hosts."

The blessings that flow from tithes are awesome:

Provision in the Church;

An open heaven

Blessings to overflowing

Protection from the enemy on our "land"

Fruitfulness for our children

Favor that can be seen by others

I want to touch on the fact that when we tithe, the "windows of heaven" will be opened to us. This is so powerful! This means that there will be a flow of revelation, light, wisdom, insight, new ideas, new strategies and angelic help on your life. Whether you are a banker, a baker, a doctor, a housewife, a businessman, an architect, an evangelist, with the windows of heaven opened over your life, there will be 20/20 vision at the eye gate! The Holy Spirit will manifest His excellence over your life, giving great glory to God! This is why I believe that believers should be the ones excelling in every area of life, because of the indwelling of the Holy Spirit.

It is not by "accident" that it was Cornelius, a Roman centurion, the one chosen by God, in whose house the gospel was preached to the Gentiles for the first time. He was a generous man! In Acts 10, we find the account of how the Holy Spirit moved to have the gospel preached to the Gentiles in Cornelius's home. Three times in this chapter the Holy Spirit makes the point that Cornelius was a generous man:

> "At Caesarea there was a man named Cornelius... a devout man who feared God with all his household, and gave alms liberally to the people, and prayed constantly to God." (Acts 10:1-2).

Cornelius was visited by an angel who told him this:

> "...Cornelius...your prayers and your alms have ascended as a memorial before God." (Acts 10:3-4).

> "...Cornelius, your prayer has been heard and your alms have been remembered before God." (Acts 10:31).

The Lord is the master accountant! A record of our giving is kept before Him as a memorial!

There is something about generosity that touches the heart of God! It's His character: He is generous! We honor Him when we tithe and give our offerings. He is the One who set the pattern:

> "For God so loved the world that He gave his only Son...." (John 3:16).

One of the characteristics of the early Church was its generosity:

> "And all who believed were together and had all things in common; and they sold their possessions and goods and distributed them to all, as any had need." (Acts 2:44-45).

> "There was not a needy person among them, for as many as were possessors of lands or houses sold them, and brought the proceeds of what was sold and laid it at the apostles' feet; and distribution was mad to each as any had need." (Acts 4:34-35).

Imagine, not a needy person in their midst! The Church was taking care of their poor: orphans, widows, the unemployed. In this atmosphere of generosity, the Holy Spirit moved in great power! When the Lord becomes Lord of our finances, He really has a hold of our hearts! When He gets hold of our hearts, He can do anything He wants with us and through us! "Great grace" (Acts 4:33) and "great power" (Acts 4:33) will once again be manifested through the Church! Can't wait!

> "He who gives to the poor will not want, but he who hides his eyes will get many a curse." (Proverbs 28:27).

My daughter has been faithfully tithing. She lives in New York and needed to come back home to sell her car. We agreed in prayer that she would receive $6,000 for her car. She sold her car at $7,500 and in addition her godparents gave her an additional $1,000. She came back home expecting $6,000, but she left with $8,500. This is God! He cannot be outdone in generosity!

> "...give, and it will be given to you; good measure, pressed down, shaken together, running over...."
> (Luke 6:38).

IX

HOW CAN WE SEE?

"And their eyes were opened and they recognized Him…." (Luke 24:31).

It is the Holy Spirit that unveils our eyes so that we can "see" Jesus and the things of God. He is the spirit of revelation; He is the One who enlightens our hearts. The Apostle Paul prays in Ephesians 1:17-19:

> "that the God of our Lord Jesus Christ, the Father of glory, may give you a spirit of wisdom and of revelation in the knowledge of Him, having the eyes of your hearts enlightened, that you may know what is the hope to which he has called you, what are the riches of his glorious inheritance in the saints, and what is the immeasurable greatness of his power in us who believe…."

This apostolic prayer of St. Paul is a great prayer for us, our children, our families, our Church! We need our eyes to continually open to what the Holy Spirit wants to show us, so that we can partner with Him to extend God's kingdom on earth and enforce the victory of Calvary everywhere that we go.

I say it's time to surrender our hearts to the Lord so that we can learn His ways:

> "My son, give me your heart, and let your eyes observe my ways." (Proverbs 23:26).

The Lord tells the Church of Laodicea that they are blind and counsels them to buy "salve to anoint your eyes, that you may see." (Revelation 3:17, 20).

It's time for us, the Church, to buy eye salve and anoint our eyes so that we may see!

These are some important ways in which we can "buy" eye salve so that we may see.

The WORD OF GOD:

"Is not my word like fire, says the Lord, and like a hammer which breaks the rock in pieces?"

The word of God is like a hammer that shatters the strongholds of wrong thinking in our minds (2 Corinthians 10:4-5). All of us have strongholds that need to be pulled down because our thinking and believing are not in agreement with the Word of God; we have been believing lies even without knowing it! These lies come from different sources: our culture, our ethnic background, our family, our schools, the devil (who is the father of lies!) (John 8:44). They keep us blind to the truth until the Holy Spirit, the Spirit of Truth, enters in with the truth of God's Word to replace the lie. We must "take every thought captive to obey Christ..." (2 Corinthians 10:5). Things like prejudice and racism, self-hatred, self-pity, fear, for example, are rooted in lies and those strongholds need to come down! All of us have believed lies about ourselves that are not true! If God's kingdom is not foremost in your life and you are not carrying on with the works of Jesus, then you need to correct your vision! Ask the Lord to open your eyes with His Word!

> "Open my eyes, that I may behold wondrous things out of thy law." (Psalm 119:18).

> "Thy Word is a lamp to my feet and a light to my path." (Psalm 119:105).

> "The unfolding of thy words gives light; it imparts understanding to the simple." (Psalm 119:130).

"…the commandment of the Lord is pure, enlightening the eyes…." (Psalm 19:8).

"For the commandment is a lamp and the teaching a light…." (Proverbs 6:23).

"So faith comes from what is heard, and what is heard comes by the preaching of Christ." (Romans 10:17).

It is through the preaching of the Word of God that the veils blinding our eyes to the truth of the Gospel are taken away. The enemy is an expert in keeping people in darkness:

"…the god of this world has blinded the minds of the unbelievers, to keep them from seeing the light of the gospel of the glory of Christ, who is the likeness of God." (2 Corinthians 4:4).

In 2006 I ministered with a team in a remote place in Uganda called Kotido. We preached, ministered, healed, delivered; hundreds of people gave their lives to Jesus and received the baptism of the Holy Spirit. After three years I went back to the same place and rejoiced in seeing the fruit from our ministry. I want to share one woman's testimony from that outreach. This lady told me:

"Three years ago when you came to the church, I was just sitting there, hopeless and not understanding anything because I did not speak English. I had no purpose and meaning in my life and thought I was good for nothing. But you prayed over me and asked the Holy Spirit to come; you also said that I was anointed to proclaim the gospel. My life totally changed since then! Now, I am speaking English and I'm telling people about Jesus everywhere I go, without fear! I go to the prison to proclaim the good news and I'm being trained as a catechist."

This lady is full of joy and she is a living testimony of God's grace! When the truth of the Word of God shattered her strongholds and she believed, her life changed!

If we don't know the truth, the Word of God, we will believe the lies! Ask the Lord to give you a love for the Truth!

I was encouraged by Pope Benedict's words at the close of 2009 and the beginning of 2010; he encouraged Catholics to make a New Year's resolution to spend more time reading the Bible so that we could become more credible witness to God's loving plan of salvation.

(Taken from Spiritdaily website on January 1, 2010). Praise the Lord!

EUCHARIST:

"Jesus said to them, I Am the bread of life...." (John 6:35).

On the road to Emmaus, confused and with a veil over their eyes, the disciples' eyes were opened as Jesus "took the bread and blessed, and broke it, and gave it to them." (Luke 24:30). Are you confused or blind regarding certain things in your life or your faith? Allow the Lord to open your eyes as you partake of Holy Communion with Him. In that time of intimacy with the Lord, allow the Holy Spirit to open your eyes where you need vision. Intimacy with the Lord is part of our birthright. It releases revelation. Talk to the Lord, open the doors of your heart to Him, unload all your worries; listen to His voice. Your "yes" and your surrender is what He is looking for! Let "rivers" of grace flood your being at that moment so that we can say like Mary,

"...let it be to me according to Your word." (Luke 1:38).

To the Church of Laodicea the Lord said:

"Behold, I stand at the door and knock; if any one hears my voice and opens the door, I will come in to him and eat with him, and he with me." (Revelation 3:20).

The Lord still knocks at the door of our hearts! It's a continuous opening of our hearts; as we partake of the Eucharist it is a perfect moment to allow Jesus into the depths of our being and have intimacy with Him. "Be still, and know that I am God.

(Psalm 46:10). We receive Jesus in the Eucharist; therefore we are receiving the Holy Spirit! Receive Him in a worthy manner. St. Paul says in 1 Corinthians 11:27-30:

> "Whoever, therefore, eats the bread or drinks the cup of the Lord in an unworthy manner will be guilty of profaning the body and blood of the Lord. Let a man examine himself, and so eat of the bread and drink of the cup. For any one who eats and drinks without discerning the body eats and drinks judgment upon himself. That is why many of you are weak and ill, and some have died."

These are tough words, but we need to hear them. To partake of the Eucharist is a big blessing, but it can turn into the opposite if we are not receiving Him in a worthy manner.

TESTIMONY:

> "And they have conquered him by the blood of the Lamb and by the word of their testimony…."
> (Revelation 12:11).

Testimony is one of the biggest "eye-openers" that we have. This is really using our tongue for life and victory (Proverbs 18:21). It's crucial that we understand the importance that our testimony has in the spiritual realm, so that we use every available opportunity to give glory to God and extend His Kingdom on earth. Testimony releases the power of God to do the same thing that the person is testifying about; it releases realms of victory for the people listening. Eyes open, faith increases and it's a perfect set-up for the Holy Spirit to do mighty things!

The Samaritan woman who encountered Jesus in John 4, went back to her city and gave testimony. This is what happened:

> "Many Samaritans from that city believed in him because of the woman's testimony…." (John 4:39).

I was invited to have dinner with several young couples. One of the young men there had just had knee surgery; he was in pain and was not able to walk properly. I totally forgot about it as we sat down for dinner; I proceeded to give testimonies of many miracles that the Lord had done in Africa. I mentioned how a teenager that had been paralyzed, not only walked, but ran! One of the men present said, "If only I see those miracles with my eyes, I will believe!" After dinner we prayed and as everyone was getting up out of their chairs, the young man with the knee problem had received a healing! He was all excited and certainly very surprised as he moved his knee without pain! The Holy Spirit confirmed the word of the testimony that had come out of my mouth by healing someone's knee! I said to the young man that had expressed unbelief "You see, a miraculous healing just took place in your own living room, right in front of your eyes! The Lord is calling you to believe!"

PRAISE AND WORSHIP:

"Yet thou are holy, enthroned on the praises of Israel." (Psalm 22:3).

As we praise the Lord, we build Him a "throne" in which He can sit and extend His rule. One of the many things that the Holy Spirit does in times of praise and worship is release revelation so that we can see. Part of His job description is opening the eyes of the blind. Everyone has areas of blindness; we must allow the Lord to reveal to us the "logs" in our eyes so that we can see clearly.

"...the Lord opens the eyes of the blind...." (Psalm 146:8).

He also wants to guide us and show us new things to come. Jesus said in John 16:13,

"When the Spirit of truth comes, he will guide you into all the truth; for he will not speak on his own authority, but whatever he hears he will speak, and he will declare to you the things that are to come."

Last month in Agape Centre, Tanzania, we praised and worshiped the Lord with all of our being. The night sessions were just praise and worship and we allowed the Holy Spirit to have His way. On the first night, a young priest was there, watching what was going on; he remained on the sidelines. The second night he was there again; this time he fully immersed himself in the presence of the Lord, praising the Lord with all of his being. The following morning in Mass he gave a powerful testimony of how the Lord ministered to him during the praise and worship the night before. He shared that he had been preparing to give a retreat that weekend, and during the times of praise and worship the Lord gave him a download of all the talks he had to give! By revelation from the Holy Spirit he received the themes of his talks! He was so happy and grateful to the Lord!

During times of praise and worship, we develop the "eyes" of a dove, so that we can keep our eyes fixed on Jesus and not on the circumstances. In that atmosphere, the Lord also gives us the "eyes" of an eagle, so that we can see the end from the beginning. Our spiritual vision gets adjusted so that we have 20/20 vision in the Spirit:

"…for I am God, and there is no other; I am God, and there is none like me, declaring the end from the beginning…." (Isaiah 46:9-10).

Knowing the end from the beginning gives us strength to "cross" to the other side!

Brothers and sisters, we need to catch the "revelation" that as we praise the Lord, He fights for us! Our "high praises" become two-edged swords in our hands to bind the enemy, drive him away and execute judgment on him! (Psalm 149:6-9).

Our heavenly Father is looking for worshippers! Jesus said it:

> "But the hour is coming, and now is, when the true worshippers will worship the Father in spirit and truth, for such the Father seeks to worship him. God is spirit, and those who worship him must worship in spirit and truth." (John 4:23-24).

Our praise and worship does not make God any bigger or better than He already is! HE IS THE GREAT I AM from all eternity! We are the ones that are changed in His presence (1 Corinthians 3:17); we are the ones who benefit from spending time with him. It's in His presence that we are changed and that is what He wants: that His children look like Jesus! It's in His presence that He fights for us; it's in His presence that we are healed, delivered, set free!

A good friend of mine was having a tough financial time during 2009. Her husband is a developer and the houses that their company had built were not selling, as people were not spending money. They had over twenty homes that needed to sell! She was full of fear and anxiety; she wasn't too sure that Papa wanted to help her. I told her to move in faith and start thanking and praising her heavenly Father in advance. She attended the WOW conference in Boston, "Warriors of Worship," where we spent lots of time in God's presence in praise and worship. Within two weeks after the conference they had sold fifteen homes! WOW! What a testimony!

X

THE ABUNDANT LIFE IS YOURS!

"I came that they may have life, and have it abundantly." (John 10:10).

Living a rested, joyful life in Christ are two of the biggest blessings available for every believer. No matter what we go through, we can remain in the rest and joy of the Lord! That will truly help us focus on the vision the Lord has for us and is a great witness to unbelievers.

ENTER INTO THE REST OF THE LORD

"For thus said the Lord God, the Holy One of Israel,
In returning and rest you shall be saved;
In quietness and in trust shall be your strength."
(Isaiah 30:15).

The Lord is trustworthy and He can be trusted with every detail of our lives; we need to rest in this truth!

"God is not man, that he should lie, or a son of man, that he should repent. Has he said, and will he not do it? Or has he spoken, and will he not fulfill it?" (Numbers 23:19).

Either we believe the Scriptures and live the abundant life (John 10:10) Jesus came to bring to us, or we'll live like the people of the world, gripped by insecurity, selfish ambition, the need to control, fear, anxiety, panic attacks, depression, sin. It was unbelief that prevented the Israelites from entering into their rest:

> "So we see that they were unable to enter because of unbelief." (Hebrews 2:19).

It is unbelief that keeps us from possessing the inheritance the Lord won for us at Calvary, thereby keeping us outside His rest. The Lord wants us to leave behind the "land of unbelief, striving and anxiety" and enter into His rest. Look at what the Lord told His people after they possessed their promise, the promised land:

> "I gave you a land on which you had not labored, and cities which you had not built, and you dwell therein; you eat the fruit of vineyards and olive yards which you did not plant." (Joshua 24:13).

The Lord freely gave them land in which someone else labored; gave them cities built by others; vineyards and olive yards that were planted by others. It had already been promised by God while in their desert wanderings. Moses told them that the Lord would give them

> "...great and goodly cities, which you did not build, and houses full of all good things, which you did not fill, and cisterns hewn out, which you did not hew, and vineyards and olive trees, which you did not plant...."
> (Deuteronomy 6:10-11).

God's people just had to believe, receive and possess! It's the same for us! Jesus has already paid the price for everything that we need on the cross of Calvary for us to live a supernatural life on earth:

He took our sin so that we could be forgiven and we would become the righteousness of God. (2 Corinthians 5:21).

He took on Himself all the sickness and disease so that we could be healed. (Isaiah 53:4-5).

He took our poverty so that we could experience His abundance. (2 Corinthians 8:9).

He became a curse so that we could enter into the blessing of Abraham. (Galatians 3:13-14).

He took our shame so that we could experience His glory. (Psalm 69:7; John 17:22).

He took our rejection and abandonment so that we could be adopted into God's family. (Matthew 27:46; Ephesians 1:5).

It's already a done deal! From the Cross Jesus said "It is finished…." (John 19:30). Every victory, breakthrough, provision, healing is already provided for in the Spirit realm. By faith we believe, receive, and approppriate! This is why the enemy attacks our minds with doubt, because if we don't believe what God says is true, we won't enter into His rest. Entering into His rest does not mean that we become passive; on the contrary, from the position of rest we battle and enforce the victory that Jesus has already won for us. The rest of the Lord is released as we abide in Him.

"By this we know that we abide in him and he in us, because he has given us of his own Spirit." (1 John 4:13).

It's only by abiding in Him that we bear eternal fruit (John 15:4-5). No matter what we go through in life, as we keep abiding in Him we will bear fruit and experience His rest. We don't necessarily bear fruit and experience rest from the circumstances or by the things we do; it's by abiding in Him! In my own life, when my marriage broke and we lost our finances, and I suddenly became a single mother, I realized that I had to remain abiding in the Lord or I would die! The only reason I could sleep at night without sleeping pills and function throughout the day without prescription drugs was because Jesus was in control of my life; as I abided in Him, He gave me what I needed every step of the way. By His grace I was able to keep focused on Him and His plan for my life during very difficult and dark moments, and today I can say, like the Apostle Paul, that,

"…I count everything as loss because of the surpassing worth of knowing Christ Jesus my lord…." (Philippians 3:8).

In Acts 12, we find Peter imprisoned; Herod had plans to kill him that night:

> "The very night when Herod was about to bring him out, Peter was sleeping between two soldiers, bound with two chains…." (Acts 12:6).

Peter was sleeping! As a matter of fact, he was sleeping so soundly that when an angel of the Lord was sent to rescue him, the angel had to wake him up in spite that "a light shone on the cell." (v.7). The angel

> "struck Peter on the side and woke him…." (v.7).

What did Peter have that enabled him to rest peacefully in spite of his circumstances? He had Jesus! He trusted the Lord! Many people today can't even sleep in the comfort of their own beds because of fear, worry and anxiety. They consume many types of pills and medication that put them to sleep, but these pills don't go to the root of the problem; they only deal with the symptoms. Jesus is the One that sets us free and gives us rest:

> "Come to me, all who labor and are heavy laden, and I will give you rest. Take my yoke upon you, and learn from me; for I am gentle and lowly in heart, and you will

> find rest for your souls. For my yoke is easy and my burden is light." (Matthew 11:28-30).

The Lord's yoke is easy and His burden is light! When we are yoked to the Lord, He is the One carrying the weight, doing the job of pulling and leading; we just need to let Him do it. Anything else we are yoked to that is not the Lord is a hard "taskmaster!" (Exodus 1:11). Check yourself whether you are "rested" or "heavy laden." Rest is something unique to God's people; it makes us

> "distinct…from all other people that are upon the face of the earth." (Exodus 33:16).

LIVE IN THE JOY OF THE LORD!

> "…I overflow with joy in all our troubles."
> (2 Corinthians 7:4b) (Douay Version).

The Apostle Paul overflowed with joy in the midst of all his troubles! It was not a little trickle of joy, but it was a "river of joy" that overflowed from his innermost being. Jesus was his joy! No matter what he went through, he trusted the Lord and stayed connected to his source of joy.

We need to change our perspective regarding trials and tribulations! Instead of grumbling and complaining or running away, the Lord thinks that we should rejoice:

> "Count it all joy, my brethren, when you meet various trials…." (James 1:2).

Why would James say this? Why should we rejoice when we face trials, tribulations and adversity? Look at verses 3 and 4:

> "…for you know that the testing of your faith produces steadfastness. And let steadfastness have its full effect, that you may be perfect and complete, lacking in nothing."

Ultimately, every trial, tribulation, adversity that comes your way is meant to produce strong faith and character in you; you are being equipped to conquer and experience victory. Through the trials and tribulations our "faith muscles" are developed so that we mature from children to sons/daughters of God. Remember, that "...without faith it is impossible to please him" (Hebrews 11:6).

So it's your choice to rejoice! Can you "see" it? And as you do so, you remain strong in the Lord, because

> "...the joy of the Lord is your strength." (Nehemiah 8:10).

You can't let the enemy steal your joy! He didn't give it to you in the first place, the Lord did! Jesus said,

> "...and no one will take your joy from you." (John 16:22).

Joy is part of our inheritance in Christ Jesus; it's fruit of the Holy Spirit (Galatians 5:22), Who lives inside of us. Joy is also found in the presence of the Lord:

> "...in thy presence there is fullness of joy, in thy right hand are pleasures forevermore." (Psalm 16:11).

No matter what you are going through, as you learn to praise your way through the problems, trials and tribulation, you enter into the joy of the Lord. Psalm 100: 4 says,

> "Enter his gates with thanksgiving, and his courts with praise!"

First step into his presence: thanksgiving. Second step is to move into praise; as He inhabits our praises (Psalm 22:3), the response is to worship! There in His presence is "fullness of joy!"

Praise changes the atmosphere and the enemy has to flee: tormenting spirits, depression, anxiety, fear, panic attacks, etc. There will be a download of revelation for your situation. When we praise the Lord we focus on Him, His greatness, His power,

His faithfulness, etc.; we stop looking at the problem and instead we look at Him. The Lord becomes our reality, not the "stuff" that we are going through! We remember that our God is bigger than our problem! He has a plan, a strategy, a solution to get us out. What we are going through is temporary, and as we fix our eyes on Him and His kingdom, our perspective changes. St. Paul says that

> "for this slight momentary affliction is preparing for us an eternal weight of glory beyond all comparison…."
> (2 Corinthians 4:17).

All the trials and difficulties that we go through is creating for us a weight of glory that we will carry so that we can release His glory everywhere that we go. Joy will become more and more desirable as the days get darker and trouble increases. As God's people, we don't have to live like the people in the world, gripped with fear, anxiety, depression, because like Job, we can say

> "for I know that my Redeemer lives…." (Job 19:25).

The Lord conquered at the Cross! He resurrected and He sits on the throne! He is not worried about a thing! Why should we?

We are in the world but not of the world; we are kingdom people and have received a kingdom that cannot be shaken. What happened in Egypt during the plagues that God sent, that Goshen (where God's people lived) was protected and spared from those plagues, is going to happen to us. Everyone will be able to see the difference between God's people and the people of the world as we remain steadfast in His joy! In the days ahead, God's people will be radically different from the people in the world! We will have joy and peace, unlike the rest of the people that don't know the Lord and are stressed out, gripped with fear, anxiety, depression. Joy will become a "bait" that will draw many to Jesus when they see it on us!

Jesus was anointed with the "oil of gladness" beyond anyone else! (Hebrews 1:9). He had a very attractive, joyful personality that drew many people to Him. Shouldn't we resemble that aspect of His character? Shouldn't the bride of Christ be filled with the oil of gladness more than any one else, since we have such a Lovely, Wonderful, Caring, Faithful Bridegroom? Part of the Messiah's anointing was

> "to grant to those who mourn in Zion—
> To give them a garland instead of ashes, the oil of
>   gladness instead of mourning,
> The mantle of praise instead of a faint spirit...."

I say it's time to trade our "faint spirit" for a "mantle of praise!" It's your choice to rejoice!

> "For the kingdom of God does not mean food and drink but righteousness and peace and joy in the Holy Spirit." (Romans 14:17).

RELEASE THE GLORY!

> "...all the earth shall be filled with the glory of the Lord...." (Numbers 14:21).

It is God's desire that all the earth be filled with His glory. What exactly is the "glory?"

If the glory can be narrowed down to one word (which it really can't), it's this: His goodness!

Moses asked the Lord to show him His glory:

> "I pray thee, show me thy glory. And he said, I will make all my goodness pass before you, and will proclaim before you my name...." (Exodus 33:18-19).

What would "all the goodness" of God include?

I believe it includes all the blessings of the Kingdom! All the blessings that flow out of His mercy and grace: salvation, healing, deliverance, love, joy, peace, restoration, miracles, extra-ordinary miracles, provision, etc. The glory includes His majesty and splendor; His generosity, everything that He is!

Who's supposed to fill the earth with the glory of God? You and me! We are carriers of the glory because we house the Holy Spirit! The kingdom of God is within us! It seems that all of creation knows who we are except us! Paul writes,

> "For the creation waits with eager longing for the revealing of the sons of God...." (Romans 8:19).

The whole of creation is waiting for God's people to rise up and carry on with the works of Jesus! Where there is sickness and disease, to release healing; where there is misery, to destroy the works of the devil; where there is injustice, to release justice; where there is depression and hopelessness, to release joy and hope! We are supposed to impact and change our surroundings!

The problem is that we are suffering from an identity crises; but not for long! The Holy Spirit is moving and awakening God's people to rise up and move into its rightful place as a conquering, fearless people ready to enforce the victory of Calvary over every demonic stronghold holding God's people captive. The Lord is raising a generation of warrior/worshipers that spend time in God's glorious presence and are eager to extend the kingdom wherever they go. Can you "see" it?

The Lord has always wanted to "tabernacle" with His people. He asked Moses to build a tabernacle in the wilderness where He could dwell; David raised a tabernacle quite different than Moses' on Mt. Zion; Solomon built him a temple.

Then the Father sent Jesus, who

> "reflects the glory of God and bears the very stamp of his nature...." (Hebrews 1:3).

Jesus is the glory of God and the revelation of the goodness of God!

John writes,

> "...we have beheld his glory, glory as of the only Son from the Father," (John 1:14).

After Jesus ascended to the Father, the Father gifted Him with the Holy Spirit, and Jesus gave us His gift! On Pentecost day, Peter said about Jesus in Acts 2:33,

> "Being therefore exalted at the right hand of God, and having received from the Father the promise of the Holy Spirit, he has poured out this which you see and hear."

> What a gift the Holy Spirit is! He is the Spirit of glory! (1 Peter 4:14) and He lives in us!

> Jesus told the Father:

> "The glory which thou has given me I have given to them...." (John 17:22).

The glory belongs to the Lord! But He has chosen us to partake of His glory so that His goodness can be released through us to win a lost humanity to Him! Last week in the gym I was talking to a very nice lady whom the Lord has healed several times of different aches and pains. She also has opened her heart to Jesus as Lord and Savior. We were on the treadmill, engaged in conversation, when suddenly she said, "As I am talking to you, all the pain I had in my right shoulder has left me!" "Healing glory" healed her shoulder! There will be an increasing manifestation of God's glory in the days ahead; just like the Apostle Peter in Acts 5:14-16, as we release God's glory, many will be healed and set free through us. Glory to God!

Brothers and sisters, we have been equipped to release His glory, which is His goodness!

As we set out to fulfill the Great Commission, the glory of God will be released through us! As we demonstrate the power of the Gospel, we will release His glory and goodness and will see many people repent and turn to the Lord, because

> "...the goodness of God is meant to lead thee to repentance...."
> (Romans 2:4) (The Holy Bible, Douay Version).

As the Gospel of the Kingdom is proclaimed and its power demonstrated, I have never failed to see people repent and turn to the Lord once they see the goodness and glory of God. It is the promise of God that as we go, He works with us and confirms the message with signs and wonders (Mark 16:20).

Brothers and sisters, this could be the finest hour of the Church, if we just wake up and assume our position as the people of God on earth. We can't remain passive at this time. Increasing darkness must be viewed from God's perspective: it is an opportunity to release the light of Christ and make Jesus known and loved:

> "Arise, shine; for your light as come, and the glory of the Lord has risen upon you.
> For behold, darkness shall cover the earth, and thick darkness the peoples;
> But the Lord will arise upon you and his glory will be seen upon you.
> And nations shall come to your light, and kings to the brightness of your rising.
> Lift up your eyes round about, and see…."
> (Isaiah 60:1-4).

I say it's time for the Church to wake up, rise up and "step up to the plate!"

Dear reader, I hope this book has helped you to understand how important it is to protect our eye gate, so that we can see as God sees. Our eyes belong to God! As a prophetic people, we are to walk by revelation so that we can be "light" in the midst of darkness! We have been empowered to carry on with the works of Jesus and we are not alone in this; we partner with the Holy Spirit! Step into what the Lord has assigned for you! There is a unique plan and purpose for your life; enter into it, knowing

> "that he who began a good work in you will bring it to completion…." (Philippians 1:6).

Some of you are called to go to the nations, to open orphanages, nursing homes, day-care centers, even schools, in order to fulfill our mandate to proclaim the good news to every creature! Some of you are called to hold high level government positions; some of you are called to impact the medical world, our financial institutions, the entertainment world and even the mass media with the gospel of the kingdom! Whatever the Lord has assigned to you, go for it! Don't give up!

> "Not to him who is able to keep you from falling and to present you without blemish before the presence of his glory with rejoicing, to the only God, our Savior through Jesus Christ our Lord, be glory, majesty, dominion, and authority, before all time and now and for ever. Amen" (Titus 24-25).

Prayer of salvation:

"Lord, this day I come before you repenting for my sin. Lord Jesus, I believe that You are the Son of God and that You died for my sins on the Cross of Calvary. Forgive me, Lord, and cleanse me now with Your precious blood. I renounce sin, satan and his lies. I invite You to come into my life as my Lord and my Savior. I confess with my mouth that Jesus is Lord and that God raised Him from the dead. I thank You, Lord, for the gift of salvation and eternal life. Fill me now with Your Holy Spirit and help me to live for you."

About the Author

Born in Havana, Cuba, **Maria Vadia** was 10 years old when she and her family fled to Miami, Florida to escape the communist regime in her native country. She attended Catholic schools and was a "Sunday" Catholic with no personal relationship with the Lord Jesus Christ. Later married to a wealthy man, she was gripped by materialism; yet in the midst of everything the world could offer, she knew that something was missing.

Maria was baptized in the Holy Spirit in 1987 and consecrated her life to the Lord Jesus Christ and to the preaching of the Gospel. In spite of great adversity, the Lord has been with her like a "mighty warrior" (Jeremiah 20:11).

Maria is active in the "Catholic Charismatic Renewal" of the Archdiocese of Miami and has spoken at many charismatic conferences. She is founder of the "Jesus is Lord" chapter of Magnificat in Miami, and a member of the Advisory Board of Magnificat, International, a ministry for Catholic Women. She has traveled around America, Cuba, Trinidad & Tobago, Barbados, Jamaica, Mexico, Malta, Ghana, Nicaragua, Uganda, Tanzania, Zambia, Indonesia, Papua New Guinea, Canada and India, bringing a message of faith, salvation and healing. She ministers the Word to various prayer groups, including "The King Jesus Prayer Group" which she has faithfully led since 1992, as well as at the Miami Women's Detention Center and Genesis House, a home for the homeless with AIDS (presently closed). Maria leads a weekly bible class, "Healing Through The Word," in her parish of St. Louis Catholic Church. She has authored five books; *There's Power In Your Tongue, Pressing On In The Spirit, An Arrow In His Hand, Healing Is For You,* and *Break Open Your Wells!*